CW01627436

PERSONAL *and* PROFESSIONAL *stories*

QUILTED

FROM PATTERN TO PATCHWORK

TARA FAUGHNAN

PERSONAL *and* PROFESSIONAL *stories*

QUILTED

FROM PATTERN TO PATCHWORK

TARA FAUGHNAN

ENCYCLOPEDIA OF INSPIRATION

UPPERCASE

QUILTED
VOLUME "Q"

QUILTS BY SHERRI LYNN WOOD, PHOTO BY SARAH REMINGTON FROM *THE IMPROV HANDBOOK FOR MODERN QUILTERS* (ABRAMS, 2015). THIS PAGE: JANINE VANGOOL.

encyclopediaofinspiration.com
uppercasemagazine.com

PRINTED IN CANADA BY THE PROLIFIC GROUP

WRITING & DESIGN
JANINE VANGOOL

COPYEDITING
CORREY BALDWIN

UPPERCASE PUBLISHING INC
201B – 908, 17TH AVENUE SW
CALGARY, ALBERTA, CANADA T2T 0A3

You are welcome to share photos of this book in your life on Instagram:
#encyclopediaofinspiration
#uppercasequilted
@uppercasemag

QUILT STORIES

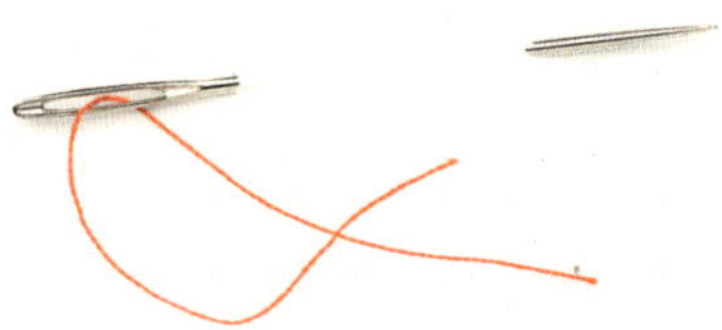

QUILTERS

MOM

Quilty by Association

by Janine Vangool

First of all, let me confess that I'm *not* a quilter. I have made one quilt from start to finish and that felt like a full-on disaster, which, in retrospect, I blame on my inexperience at not recognizing that the tension of my sewing machine was malfunctioning. This quilt now resides on my son's bed, and he doesn't mind the puckers and imprecision so I guess it wasn't a real failure after all—the only disappointment being the gulf between my expectations and reality.

I also have numerous quilts in progress: An English paper pieced hexagon design that combines vintage feed sacks with fabrics from my collections released through Windham Fabrics. It's going to take years to complete. A quilt designed for my third collection with Windham Fabrics, Circular Logic, that will also be entirely made by hand. And another machine-pieced quilt I've titled The Sunrise Quilt that I'm quilting by hand with a big stitch. There are also various patchwork pieces, improv experiments and projects that I suppose are called UFOs (unfinished objects). But that's ok. I love strolling eBay, sometimes buying UFOs from bygone eras... unfinished feed sack quilt tops being my weakness. Maybe someday my own unfinished pieces will be interesting and covetable artifacts of this time.

My love for quilts is genuine and generational. My grandmother was a professional seamstress who made drapery; she was also a quilter who made beautiful quilts and blankets from old clothes and scraps. I treasure her quilts and use them often, with just one delicate one with a white background stowed away for safekeeping. My mother is a prolific quilter as well, and I am grateful for her help in making sample quilts

OPPOSITE

The Sunrise Quilt was improvised using Sharon McConnell (page 312) of Color Girl Quilts' Classic Curves ruler.

ABOVE

Items made from my debut collection with Windham Fabrics. The low-volume quilt on the wall was made by Cheryl Arkison (page 62).

PORTRAIT BY KIRSTIE TWEED

for my fabric look books. I get my work ethic and attention to detail from her.

I have full intentions of being a quilter, someday, when I have more free time. In the meantime, I'm fortunate to be quilty by association! Through the collections I've created for Windham Fabrics, I've had the opportunity to design many quilts and see them come to life through other people's skills at assembly and pattern making. I've met many inspiring quilters in person at Quilt Markets and virtually via Instagram, many of whom are featured in this book.

The world of quilting is vast, with an infinite range of aesthetics, influences, heritage and culture. This book is but a small sampling of quilting talent—pieced together from professional connections, admiration and friendship. ✻

HERE AND THERE SQUARES DESIGNED BY JANINE VANGOOL AND MADE BY BONNIE VANGOOL. PHOTOS BY KIRSTIE TWEED.

"Quilting reminds us of the artistry and ingenuity of our ancestors and allows us to explore our natural creativity. The craft slows us down in an ever-busy world and connects us to a welcoming community of kindred spirits."

QUILTED

ALISON GLASS

I am primarily a fabric designer and business owner. I design and publish sewing patterns as a way to support the fabric lines and also as an important part of the business. More recently I have started producing and distributing finished goods featuring artwork from many of the lines. I also run an online shop. Also, I should note that I prefer the word "we." I am very lucky to work with a small team of talented and dedicated people who all do their part to bring the designs and the work to life.

As far as my personal life, I am a wife and mother. My husband and kids are lovely, thoughtful people who support my work and who are doing interesting things in their own lives.

What is your personal relationship or history with quilts? What draws you to them? What led you to the world of quilts?

I stumbled into the world of quilts. In 2007 I started a business focused on organization and space remodels for local clients. The organization component fell away after about a year as the design portion grew. I used fabric as the starting point for design plans and was using quite a bit of fabric from the quilting industry. These fabrics had more of the bright, bold aesthetic I wanted. At some point I realized that a person designs the fabric—something I hadn't thought about, although I have always loved fabric and sewing. I became very interested in the idea of designing fabric. I had ideas I wanted to see produced and love the activity of making repeat patterns.

I started learning Adobe Illustrator, making repeat patterns and putting them together into fabric collections. I made it a goal to show up to Quilt Market in the fall of 2011, met with a handful of companies

"I do sew some quilts, but most of my time is spent designing fabric, designing quilts and quilt patterns, and generally running the business."

and ended up designing fabric for Andover Fabrics. Before that time I had made one quilt block as a kid, then in my 20s a quilted bumper for my daughter's crib. It is kind of funny and maybe weird to admit, and different, that the first real, intentional quilts I made were for the purpose of showing my first fabric collection. I reflect now that maybe being uninformed was a detriment to those first collections, but I also see that it provided a freedom I might not have otherwise had. It is just my particular story.

How would you describe your style or aesthetic?

My aesthetic is saturated, spectrum-ordered colour mixed with muted neutrals. This combination lets the intense colour shine while giving the eye a place to rest. Also, in the artwork that becomes the fabric, there is often a lot of detail with personal meaning.

What are your intentions when making a quilt or starting a creative project? What thought processes do you typically go through?

My intentions generally when designing a quilt or partnering with a co-author to bring a design to publication are to make sure it is a viable product that people will enjoy and want to make for themselves. It may not be a romantic answer, but it is true—and these thought processes and decisions are what moves the business forward as sustainable.

What mindset or attitude do you think is best for quilting? How does quilting affect your mental and physical health?

I think openness and acceptance are good mindsets for quilting. From a pattern writer perspective I hope that our patterns will be open enough that people might want to use the designs in their own way, especially with colour choices and layout. This is something we try to encourage—the idea of exploration and making something that the person loves—whether it looks like the cover or not. Quilting is supposed to be fun. If a person gets joy from perfect points, that's great, go for it. If someone else prefers a more loose and free style, that's also great. It is wonderful when

people can encourage one another wherever they are at with acceptance and love.

Have you ever had a quilting or creative failure? What happened? What did you learn from it, if anything?

Rather than thinking of it as failure, these experiences are more of the process needed to work out a design. Almost everything I draw or lay out goes through iterations as I sort out what the end product needs. I can't share a specific example because it happens daily. There are certainly products that don't really take off, and that's okay—it is part of the process of moving forward.

What quilt traditions do you hold dear? What quilting conventions do you ignore or challenge?

I am not super into "the rules" and I do think there are often multiple good ways to get to a similar outcome. I think people should do what works best for them individually and in the moment. What I do hold dear is the idea of making as an outpouring of the self, and the value that an item has when it is handmade. The time a person gives to it makes it more meaningful. I also love the idea of quality. If possible, I hope people will use high-quality raw materials in their making to give as long a life as possible to these things they have invested their time in. Finally, the idea that a quilt is a useful object is very important to me. In the past this was a main reason for the making—warmth. I think it is wonderful when people use the quilts they make. Memories of making and using handmade items give another level of meaning to physical items.

In your opinion or experience, how does the act of quilting bridge the past, present and future?

It is similar to the question about quilt traditions—those same ideas of meaning, quality and usefulness—but with the idea that at best these aspects of quilting are for the purpose of bringing people together: communities of friends and of families. It is sort of like how as humans we move through life, so do handmade items, but often slower. Things that were made by or belonged to others provide a connection to the past, and provide the past with a bridge to continue as memories in the future. This is why we so often hear comments about "my grandmother's this" or "my dad's that." It is not that the thing itself is important, but the people, events and memories surrounding it are extremely important. Physical items act as reminders and sometimes informants.

Would you consider yourself as a professional within the quilting industry (i.e., you derive income from quilt-related activities)? When and how did you become a professional?

Yes. I went into the work I do in the quilting industry with the intention of it becoming an income-producing business, so I suppose since I signed a contract to design fabric in 2011, I have worked as a professional. That said, I think it takes a while to feel like a professional. I definitely felt a bit (a lot) like I was faking it for a while. When the business started to become viable I felt more like an actual professional. It is something measurable that shows growth and progress—that I was doing something that was beginning to make a difference personally.

"Relationships motivate and inspire me—the worth of people as individuals and the importance of the life they are experiencing. Specifically the relationships I have with my husband and kids intensely motivate me to do my work well. Who they are as individuals inspires me to grow, to do good work and to experience my own life—which I struggle with in the day-to-day intensity of what my work involves, and with who I am internally."

What breadth of activity and responsibilities do you have as a professional quilter?

My focus is on design, marketing and generally running the business. I sew at times, but most of my work is not actually physically quilting. In order to show the fabrics I design, we make many studio samples. Most of the samples are a combination of our sewing patterns and fabrics. I design most of the sample quilts and then we have a wonderful small team of people who sew and quilt for us and who are compensated for their work.

Do any particular ideas, objects or activities—outside of and unrelated to quilting—inform and inspire your quilting practice?

Things I see in the world—natural or made by humans—illustrate ideas and thoughts inside myself that are swirling around when I design. The artwork is often an outpouring of what is going on internally at the time I was making it. It is all very obscure to others and I kind of prefer it that way, so I share to the extent I am comfortable and keep the rest as a personal journal of sorts. ✻

WORKSPACE

I have lived in four places since starting the business. Up until our current home I have always worked in a portion of the living room. We finished the walk-up attic in our current house to serve as the studio and online shop. It works well, but as things have grown the space has become busy and full. After a couple of years I moved my workspace to a space at the bottom of the stairs that lead to the studio. I found that I prefer to work closer to my family, so that I am not separate from what is happening while working probably too many hours. It is what I am used to and it is a good choice for now. I imagine it will shift again at some point. It is also easier to concentrate on my own work outside of the activity and fullness of the studio space.

alisonglass.com
@alisonglass

Flower Shop

by **Nicole Daksiewicz**

"My friend Jess Zeigler from Threaded Quilting did this amazing longarm work. I like the retro feel of the lines and how the circles mimic the centre of the flowers." ***threadedquilting.com***

The Flower Shop quilt is a design I have tinkered around with for the past couple of years, changing the shapes and sizing until I landed on a larger block pattern that I really loved.

I have been a fan of Finnish designer Marimekko from an early age, particularly Maija Isola, who designed the simple flower print Unikko—the poppy print that they are so famous for. I love that a design created in the 1960s can have such a modern look, and how the large scale of that floral print makes such an impact. This is what I was hoping to convey with this design—simple and modern without being overly feminine. ✻

modernhandcraft.com
@modernhandcraft

ANDREA TSANG JACKSON

I am a textile artist, quilt designer, author and educator based in Halifax, Canada. As a young adult, I had trouble narrowing down a university major, so I endeavoured to study in the most interdisciplinary faculty I could find: architecture. After discovering what the world looked like through the lens of a designer, I decided that I wanted others to see the world that way, too—so I continued my studies in education. As a millennial, I worked from contract to contract in what seems like an eclectic smattering of experiences—museum exhibit design, graphic design, communications in the private and institutional sectors of architecture. But all of these wildly wonderful experiences always married design with education in one way or another.

The quilting medium called to me in a slow but deliberate way when I was expecting my first child. I don't really feel like I chose it, but rather, it chose me. Themes of place, belonging, community and agency—all very connected to architecture and design—are things I have explored and continue to explore through quilting. The immediacy of the medium and the way it was friendly to my young family, unlike other media—it just seemed to fit. In 2017, I was the artist in residence at the Canadian Museum of Immigration at Pier 21, and the project that I embarked on opened a lot of doors for me. Quilting is now my full-time chosen vocation.

"Openness in any creative pursuit, such as quilting, is absolutely key."

PORTRAIT BY EMMA POLIQUIN, PHOTOS BY DEBORAH WONG, NAOMI HILL AND QUILT PHOTOGRAPHY CO.

What is your personal relationship or history with quilts? What draws you to them? What led you to the world of quilts?

My personal history with quilts does not extend very far back. I made my first one when I was expecting my first child in 2011. To my knowledge at the time, no one else in my family quilted. It was not until a few years into my own journey that my mom showed me some hand-quilted blocks she never finished. While I was growing up, my mother sewed garments for my sister and me, but we were never really part of the process. I understand it better now from my perspective as a mother—that it was maybe important for her to keep her hobby separate from us. Because when you're a mother, you can be subsumed into that role, for better or for worse.

When I was designing a quilt for my second baby, I discovered solid fabrics and felt like maybe I had a voice in quilting that could be my own. I then stumbled upon the Modern Quilt Guild and thought, maybe this is where I belong.

"My aesthetic is crisp and clean, vibrant but not loud. I abstract intentionally accessible imagery, inviting points of connection from the viewer to spark discovery and discussion. Looking back at my body of work in the last three years, it seems a bit eclectic, but I can describe it as flexible and contextualized. Each project comes with its own language, and the common denominator is how I as an artist interpret and convey that language."

A WELL-DEFINED MISSION

I have a fairly defined mission that I use to measure all potential projects—these could be an opportunity that arises, a potential collaboration or merely an idea that pops into my head:

- To let people know what quilting is today. Everyone has an idea of what quilting is—images of their grandmother or aunties around a frame having a quilting bee. There are aspects of what we do today that echo those traditions, but it doesn't look like that anymore.
- To help people along in their creative journeys so that they see themselves as creative, to challenge them to try new things, to open their minds and to enable them to elevate their skills and confidence.
- To elevate domestic art to be equal to painting or photography or sculpture.

It seems very calculated (and it is!), but I am driven by results. At the end of a project, I want to ask "What was the point of this?" and know that I have an adequate answer that speaks to any of the three aspects of my mission. Not only does this help me move forward as an artist and businessperson, but it makes it easier to communicate what I do to people who are not in the quilting world or not in a creative field.

When did you become a professional?

In 2016, right off the bat. I was accepted into a craft fair and I needed to set up a website and business name. The business is continually evolving in its activities, such as patterns, classes, book, art making and exhibitions. I am able to contribute substantially to my overall household income but I do rely on my partner's income to support our family as well. I hope that as my practice and business grow, I could be fully self-sufficient if I ever needed to be.

What mindset or attitude do you think is best for quilting? How does quilting affect your mental and physical health?

Openness in any creative pursuit, such as quilting, is absolutely key. Whether someone is committed to it as a profession or finds it to be simply a joyous hobby, being open to new techniques and new ways of thinking about an age-old craft keeps the craft alive, and gives it a long life rather than something to be dabbled in.

When I started quilting seriously, I tried to sew every day. Often it was at 6am or late at night, but the small amount of time fed all the other areas of my life. This was the first time I understood what self-care meant and I now really care that others take care of themselves in the same way.

Sharing a passion into a community setting amplifies its impact. Having people to back you up and to encourage you is important. The accountability spurs me on and I want to do the same for others. The quilting community has made my world bigger and my heart wider. I have seen this same type of phenomenon happen to many quilters and I have a strong suspicion that they are a mentally healthy bunch because they belong to a community, are social and continue to be creative.

What quilt traditions do you hold dear? What quilting conventions do you ignore or challenge?

The tradition of quilting in community is what I hold onto tightly—the people, the quilters. Everything else I am fairly irreverent about. I appreciate tradition for bringing us to the present moment. But if I see it to be ill-fitting for the task at hand, or I see that it is hurtful or unjust in some way, I will respectfully disregard it.

One specific convention that I strive to challenge is how quilting is viewed in the public realm. People are happy to support quilts in quilting shows, history museums and folk art museums. But why aren't quilts in art museums and galleries? The boundaries around folk art, fine craft and fine art are a continual source of enquiry in my practice because I operate within all of these areas.

WORKSPACE

I have a dedicated studio space located in the attic of my 100-year-old house. We live in an urban area and because the house was built so long ago, the spaces are small. I share it with out-of-season clothes, hand-me-downs that are sized between my children, empty luggage and other not-so-curious curiosities.

Even so, I see my studio as a sanctuary; my children are not allowed up there without permission. I have about 40 square feet of working space, which means a lot of shifting around between tasks—cutting, pressing, piecing, quilting. I like that the footprint is small; I can only store so many supplies and fabric. I yearn for more but I realize that if I have even a slightly bigger space, I will fill it and still yearn for more.

What motivates and inspires you?

Women motivate me. I look at the art world and how women have had to fight for a voice, for a seat at the table, to be recognized as artists. The notion that a "legitimate" artist or artistic genius is a tortured person, up all hours of the night, sacrificing relationships for the sake of their art—what modern woman would actually operate like this and be considered successful? The definition of an artist needs to be rewritten and I want to be a part of that rewriting.

More specific to the quilting medium, I have never felt like more of a feminist than when I started delving into this genre. The distinction between "craft" and "crafts" is a gendered line. There is more work to be done to bring this discussion into focus, to right injustices and to open doors for new artists.

An endless form of inspiration is stories. I think that quilt makers are drawn to stories and often highlight the story of a person's life, their aspirations, hardships and celebrations. Individual and collective stories give life so much meaning and I will continue to draw from them. In The Here & Elsewhere Bee from Pier 21, I considered the 1,200 stories that I collected to be one of the raw materials that I moulded into a quilt.

Architecture and public space are always part of the way I think of the world and therefore how I approach my practice. Joseph Howe, a 19th-century politician from the Maritimes, famously asked, "What is for the public good?" This question guides my own work—Who is it for? What good does it serve, other than for me? How can I move others forward in their own lives? ❇

3rdstoryworkshop.com
@3rdstoryworkshop

Collaborating with an Unknown Quilter

by **Amy Granger**

I am relatively new to quilting and so far my work tends to be a bit experimental, offbeat, imperfect and bold. I'm a fan of vintage textiles and often go shopping at antique malls. I usually come across old, unfinished quilt tops and wonder, is it okay to buy them and use them? It would be interesting to combine something traditional and vintage with my modern aesthetic. But cutting into a quilt top that isn't mine makes me nervous—am I breaking some unspoken rule of quilting? Are the quilt police going to get mad at me?

I talked to a handful of quilters I respect and they agreed, if it isn't of historical significance and you retain its original use as a quilt, then you're good to go. I found this busy checkerboard quilt top and thought it was pretty but extremely busy, and it had no contrast. I thought it could use my help—it could be something more dramatic and visually interesting if I could rework it. So I bought it and stared at it for months, hesitant to cut into it until I had a very clear game plan.

I recently moved to the mountain town of Donnelly, Idaho, just south of Payette Lake, so I made that my subject matter. I created a big, strong, solid abstracted lake surrounded by the delicate but busy vintage patchwork. The contrast makes each more interesting. And that's what it feels like being on the lake: a vast and serene experience surrounded by the busyness of roads, commerce, forests and cabins. It was exciting to collaborate with an unknown artist, and it was a privilege to take something half done and discarded and give it it's due attention and a beautiful purpose. ✻

amygranger.com
@amy_granger_design_co

BILL VOLCKENING

I collect old quilts, but like any story there's more to it. I was adopted at birth by two of the most wonderful parents I could imagine. I grew up in New Jersey. When I was 14, I went away to the Peddie School and lived there during the school years through high school. As a freshman, I was six foot four inches and made the varsity swim team. A few years later, I discovered photography, and it kick-started my journey as a creative person.

I went to school at Rhode Island School of Design. After two years, I transferred to the School of Visual Arts in New York, where I earned a BFA in photography. By 1991, I'd finished graduate school at NYU and the International Center of Photography. During that time, I bought my first quilt.

My journey continued through many homes and many jobs, including a job as a masters swim coach, which brought me to Portland, Oregon, in 1998. Soon after, I was appointed US Masters Swimming editor of *SWIM Magazine*. Five years later, we created *SWIMMER Magazine*, and I continued as editor for almost five more years.

When I retired in 2009, I looked at all the quilts I had collected over the years and realized it was something more. It was a collection, and I was a collector. In the summer of 2019, I got married, for the first time, to the love of my life, Linda McLaughlin. I was busy while I waited for "the one" to come along.

LEFT Pieced quilt, c. 1970, Oregon. I found this work of art, made entirely of polyester, at a flea market in Tigard, Oregon, for $35. I didn't try to barter. I just paid and ran.

"There are many ways to approach quilts and look at them. I like to let them speak to me as much as possible, so I look at what's there—the technique, the creative choices and even the number of patches and stitches. Most quilts do not say who made them, but the quilts say things about their makers, their personalities and their lives."

A B O V E

Pieced quilt, c. 1860, Kentucky. This quilt is the first one I acquired. I bought it in 1989 from Shelly Zegart.

C L O C K W I S E

Pieced quilt, c. 1940, Texas. After I saw the Quilts of Gee's Bend exhibition in 2001, I started looking at quilts more like this one. I call it "perfectly imperfect."

Pieced quilt, c. 1865, Kentucky, made by the MacMillan family. This quilt is one of the examples that appeared in *Kentucky Quilts*, the book that resulted from the Kentucky Quilt Project, the first statewide quilt documentation project in the United States.

Pieced quilt, c. 1870, Virginia. I found this magnificent quilt on eBay.

How would you describe your collecting aesthetic?

Open. It wasn't always like that, though. When I first started collecting quilts, I wouldn't look at anything less than 100 years old. That's how old it needed to be to qualify as an antique. I collected high-end quilts from well-known dealers. But a few years into it, a couple of things happened that changed everything—I saw the Quilts of Gee's Bend at the Whitney, and I discovered eBay. The Gee's Bend exhibition was an eye-opener. The prevalent improvisational style was compelling, and it was coming from a rural Alabama community of quiltmakers descended from slaves. The quilts were perfectly imperfect, and they opened my mind to a wide variety of styles and time periods.

Eventually, I collected quilts that very few people appreciated at the time—the barely vintage quilts of the 1970s. Many of the quilts were made with polyester double knit fabric. I found them visually exciting, and thanks to polyester the colours were perfectly saturated. These quilts represented the collective body of work of millions of Americans learning how to make quilts during the great American quiltmaking revival of the 1970s—important with a capital "I"!

Would you consider yourself as a professional within the quilting industry?

I am really more philanthropist than anything. There is some income, book royalties and such, but it is hardly enough to qualify as a salary. The thing that makes me a professional in the quilting industry is that I bring a professional background in journalism and editorial work to it.

Technically I am retired, but is a writer ever really retired? I do not support myself on quilt-related income.

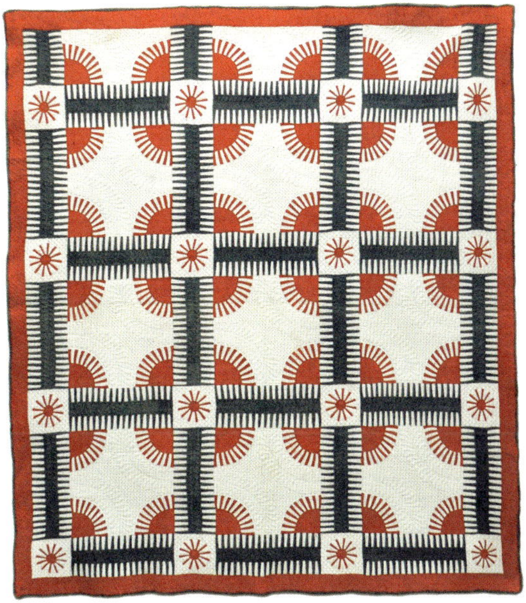

NEW YORK BEAUTY

In 1989, I started to develop a deep appreciation for quilts when I met Shelly Zegart and bought my first antique quilt from her. I fell for a stunning red, white and green Civil War–era quilt made from a design called New York Beauty.

Over the years, I collected New York Beauty quilts, and learned many things about the history of the design, such as the true origins of the popular name for the pattern. After 25 years of collecting and research, I wrote my first book, *New York Beauty: Quilts from the Volckening Collection*, published by Quiltmania in France in 2015.

Since then, I have been involved with a variety of other projects, including exhibitions, magazine articles and two more books.

LEFT

Bible Story, 1979 by Lucy Mingo, Gee's Bend, Alabama. It was part of the collection of Kyra Hicks, and before that, of Carolyn Mazloomi.

OPPOSITE

Dresden Plates, c. 1975, United States. I love how this quilt combines prints and solids to create graphic impact. The traditional design looks especially modern, with bright colours rather than pastels. I collected 1970s quilts before a lot of the other collectors realized they were collectible.

What mindset or attitude do you think is best for quilting? How does quilting affect your mental and physical health?

A peaceful, inquisitive mind is best for quilting because it can be such a zen-like activity... kind of like swimming. Of course, there are exceptions to every rule. A lot of the political quilts being made today come from a place that's not so peaceful, but the work is great. Being at peace is ultimately beneficial to my health, and that's why I engage in activities that are peaceful. Asking lots of questions keeps my mind sharp.

Have you ever had a quilting or creative failure? What happened? What did you learn from it, if anything?

Not for a long time. I made a few dreadful things while experimenting with materials and techniques in art school, and for many years I made pretty things that lacked content. Now I feel like I'm in the driver's seat, even though I don't make a lot of art objects. The thing I always learn from failure is to try again and do better the next time.

"As an infrequent maker, I like my work to be about something, even if it is a small thing. I do not use patterns, so my process is maybe a little more organic. Art school training gave me the tools to work with most any material, in various styles, so it's more about content for me."

WORKSPACE

We have a loft area in our home, and I use it to photograph quilts. The loft is basic, a white wall, some skylight, a quilt stand and a camera—a digital SLR. I do not have one designated place for my sewing machine. It doesn't get a lot of use, but I will pull it out and play from time to time.

OPPOSITE

Pieced and appliquéd quilt, c. 1975, Florida. In the 1970s, millions of Americans learned to make quilts, and originality reigned supreme. This groovy, kaleidoscopic quilt is a great example.

What quilt traditions do you hold dear? What quilting conventions do you ignore or challenge?

That's a big can of worms. I hold many of the traditions dear because they are part of the heritage of quiltmaking in America. The thing I don't like is the amount of romanticism in quilt history.

The Underground Railroad quilt code, for example, has been thoroughly debunked, but people continue to tell the story as if it is fact. The idea of Amish women including a humility block with an intentional error because "only God is perfect" is a myth. Pattern naming wasn't a thing until around the turn of the century, maybe the 1890s, when mass-media publications began including quilt patterns and marketing them. But people try to use those pattern names on older quilts, and it doesn't really work.

Another idea I always challenge is that there are singular styles of quiltmaking for various cultural groups. For example, African-American makers create all kinds of quilts, not just the improvisational style seen among the quilts of Gee's Bend. Hawaiian quiltmakers don't just make elegant, botanical appliqué quilts. They also make scrap quilts.

In your opinion or experience, how does the act of quilting bridge the past, present and future?

Quilts represent the longest unbroken chain of creative expression by women in the United States of America, and quilt history reads like an art history book. Quiltmakers invented elements of modernism in graphic design, they documented history and they kept their families warm. Styles evolved, and each new style represented a period of time just as the various styles would represent traditions in art history. As old quilts shift in function from bedcovering to artifact, there are new quilts covering the beds—and many of them will live to be old quilts... artifacts.

17 76

What motivates and inspires you?

It depends on the project or goal. Quiltmakers inspire me. Of course, a lot of my curatorial and writing projects are motivated by deadlines, but I am always inspired by what's in front of me—the quilts. "What was the maker thinking?," I wonder; and I ask, "How can their work communicate to people today? What does it have for us?"

Recently I did a small exhibit of 19th-century appliqué quilts at Latimer Quilt and Textile Center in Tillamook, Oregon. Since I was getting married in August, I wanted to do an exhibit for Linda's family—my new family. They get together for a family reunion each year in Seaside, just up the road. This exhibit was all about love—the love that went into making the quilts, and the love we feel for family and friends. I was especially motivated to show something good, knowing that bus tours would be coming from Sisters, with visitors from all around the world. It was wonderful going through the guest book and seeing how far the visitors travelled. ✻

ABOVE

Appliqué quilt, dated 1868, made by Hannah J. Swin, New Jersey. The rooster has the word "Hark" embroidered next to its beak. Appliqué quilt, c. 1850, United States. The motif in this quilt is often called a strawberry, but I believe it is actually a cardoon.

OPPOSITE

Pieced and appliqué quilt, c. 1940, Wisconsin. This bold, graphic quilt came from an eBay auction, and the seller thought it could be cut up for use in craft projects. Of course, I am doing my best to make sure people don't destroy such remarkable quilts.

RIGHT

Pieced and appliquéd quilt, c. 1975, Hawaii. Hawaii has a well-known tradition of elegant, two-colour, botanical appliqué quilts and Hawaiian flag quilts. Hawaiians also make scrap quilts, using remnants from the factories making garments such as Aloha shirts and muumuus for the tourist market.

OPPOSITE

Appliqué quilt, c. 1970, United States. This quilt came from a collector in New Mexico who found it through the Goodwill auction site. It is a quintessential rendering of the 1970s, perhaps as a child would have seen it. I had to have it, but it took several years for me to convince the other collector to sell it to me.

billvolckening.com
@billvolckening

"In most cases, we do not know who made the old quilts, but working with their designs breathes life into their work. I think that's why quiltmaking is so much more than an activity. It's a tradition, a heritage and a life cycle."

CAROLYN FRIEDLANDER

I have always loved the empowering feeling of being able to make things, whether it was drawing and making art, learning to sew or figuring out interesting things to do on the cattle and citrus ranch in central Florida where I grew up. I went on to study architecture and design in college, which clicked with me in a way that made me feel like myself. After college I learned to quilt, which became a complete obsession. For some of the same reasons I loved studying design, quilting provided the perfect platform for expressing and working through ideas. My obsession led to a decision to take my career in a direction that would allow me to work with quilts, fabric, pattern and colour.

What is your personal relationship or history with quilts? What draws you to them? What led you to the world of quilts?

I do not come from a long line of quilters, but I did grow up around sewing and other forms of craft like crochet and garment making. My mom always made clothes for me and my siblings as kids. I loved going to the fabric store with her and picking out the fabric that would go with a pattern for clothes. It was such a wild idea to see the fabric in its raw form and envision it as something entirely new and useful.

My mom started making quilts some point later, and it wasn't until I saw her doing free-motion quilting that I became intrigued with the technique. To me it looked like drawing with a sewing machine, and I was very excited about the possibilities.

"I like projects that are playful to the eye, interesting to touch and very fun and engaging to make."

"As a quilt designer, I love thinking of projects that are not only fun to make, but also perfect opportunities for quilters to express themselves. I design patterns and fabric, both of which I consider to be tools and pieces of the quiltmaking puzzle. It's my hope that people can use them to make the things they most want to make."

How would you describe your style or aesthetic?

I love working with colour and texture probably the most. I like projects that are playful to the eye, interesting to touch and very fun and engaging to make.

I've started to learn that many of my favourite colours are the ones I'm surrounded by every day—from the orange clay roads to the bright blue skies, there's definitely something about the comfort of your surroundings!

Function and process are both big things I think about in my work. I'm drawn to certain techniques and what they can allow you to do. I also enjoy thinking about how something will be used, worn or enjoyed. That can help make some decisions too.

What are your intentions when making a quilt or starting a creative project? What thought processes do you typically go through?

Most ideas come from things I've seen or ideas that I want to see how they'll turn out. I'm super visual, so I'm often starting with a sketch and then quickly

getting out some fabric and working up an idea. I have to physically work through the steps to understand it better. Making a quilt gives you many opportunities to explore an idea through the fabric, the pattern, the colours and the textures. I often find myself making multiple versions of the same project, just because I'm curious to see the results of making changes to some of the variables. Quilting is an exciting, engaging and inspiring process.

What mindset or attitude do you think is best for quilting? How does quilting affect your mental and physical health?

I think it's best to approach quilting or any creative endeavour with curiosity. I find that the projects I am most excited about and satisfied by are the ones where I was curious about how they would turn out. Whether it's how shapes can be repeated or how colours can come together, the curiosity of how it will work out is massively motivating.

Quilting can be very overwhelming, especially if you're new to it. There are a lot of variables at play,

"Gaining a better understanding of a project or technique through practice inspires me."

choices to make and techniques to get comfortable with. Sometimes it's best to fight the feeling of being overwhelmed and work with whatever feels good. It's good to remind yourself that everything gets better with practice.

I feel like quilting can both help me clear my head when I'm feeling stressed, and help fill it up with creative ideas to explore. If I'm ever lacking ideas, I find that sewing can help get those wheels turning.

Quilting can be physical, but I think for me I need to remember to stretch, take breaks to walk around, and decompress when I find myself hunched over the sewing machine too long or cramped up in a ball doing handwork.

Have you ever had a quilting or creative failure? What happened? What did you learn from it, if anything?

I have quilting failures all of the time! I like trying new things to see if they'll work, and sometimes they don't work. That's just the nature of it. The good thing about that is that you learn more about the materials and the process, which is really valuable.

I experiment a lot with batting and the layers of a quilt. I love the texture and weight of a finished project, and so I'm always tinkering with the variables to see what all you can do. Sometimes these experiments go wrong. I've layered battings that became way too weighty, and I've tried others that have been way too light. You don't know until you try!

In your opinion or experience, how does the act of quilting bridge the past, present and future?

I love thinking about quilts made in the past and the quiltmakers who made them. A neat thing about quilts is how at each step of the process, you can make decisions that will result in a totally different quilt, whether it's with the fabric, the pattern or the quilting itself.

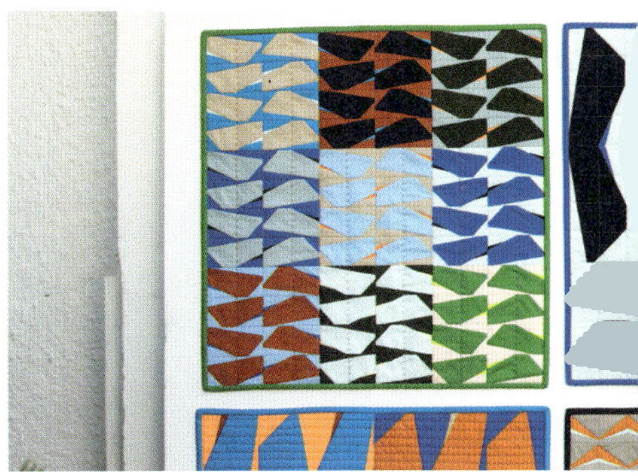

I see each quilt as a personal reflection of the maker.

In my local quilting group of friends, we span several generations. Helen was born in 1923 and was an important part of our group. When she passed away in 2018, it was a huge loss for all of us, and I was especially sad to lose her perspective. Helen came from a totally different school of quilting. She felt most comfortable using her old Singer sewing machine rather than her new computerized one, her stash was a trip back in time and she always had the most incredible comments when I'd show her my projects. She didn't know why I quilted anything more than was functionally necessary (I sometimes like a lot of quilting), and her favourite line was to ask the intended purpose for the quilt. Everything needed a purpose. I loved that she always made me think of things in new ways, and I loved seeing her life experiences and choices reflected in her projects. Quilting can tell us a lot about each other, and it can help us connect in ways that really mean something.

When and how did you become a professional? What breadth of activity and responsibilities do you have as a professional quilter?

I launched my business in the industry in 2011 by exhibiting at the Quilt Market trade show. I presented my first quilt patterns and sought to build relationships with other companies in the industry.

I support myself by working in the quilt industry. My work in the industry includes several things. I publish my own quilt patterns, design fabric collections with Robert Kaufman and have a published book with Lucky Spool Media, as well as contribute in other ways.

I love collaborating with other designers and makers, and I sometimes teach. ❋

FINDING INSPIRATION

I enjoy being outside working in my yard, going on walks and visiting new places. As well as just taking a break, seeing both the familiar and unfamiliar can spark ideas. Sometimes you need to stop thinking about something in order to find clarity about it. I can easily get stuck overthinking something, and I have to remind myself to step away in order to make it better.

WORKSPACE

To be honest, my current studio space has been under construction over the last couple of years. I'm finally nearing the end of it, but working in a changing environment and in new spaces has made me think differently about my work, as well as about how much the place where I do my work has an impact.

I love having a dedicated space to make things. I've found that when I do not have a dedicated space, I make fewer things. It just makes it easier to run with an idea when it's not a huge ordeal to get everything set up.

My studio is full of good light and lots of space for me to spread out my projects. I'm the type of person who needs to see everything in order to know that it's there. This isn't always the best quality because it can result in a lot of things being out! If things are hidden away, I tend to forget about them. My biggest studio struggle is keeping things organized and put away, but not too put away to the point where I forget about them. I'm still working on that system.

"My favourite thing about quilting is how many different ways there are to do it. If something doesn't feel right, you can always change things up to make it better.

Lately, I've found myself wanting to explore more techniques, traditional patterns and other ways of working. It can be easy to make things the way you like to make them, but I've found that seeing other ways to do things can help you find good tricks that can cross over to other things. I like connecting those dots."

carolynfriedlander.com
@carolynfriedlander

Steal Away to Jesus

by **Eliza Hardy Jones**

ABOVE

The Gee's Bend Quilt Collective building.

Mary Ann Pettway, director of the Gee's Bend Quilt Collective, sitting in front of a quilt made by Bettie Bendolph-Seltzer.

I developed the Song Quilt project in early 2016 as a way to explore how women's voices and traditional women's work connect us, challenge us, lift us up and help us understand who we are. Each song quilt visually interprets a folk song from the American South or the Russian Arctic. I was lucky enough to travel across the US and northwest Russia, interviewing women and gathering their songs and stories. From these field recordings, I create visual transcriptions of the folk songs shared with me, using a notation method I invented that translates pitch into colour, and rhythm into shape. The quilt notations are direct transcriptions of each woman's song. The quilting designs are reflections of regional textile traditions. The result is a series of 10 quilts that are a synesthetic meditation on the power of women's voices and folk traditions among diverse peoples.

The song quilt featured here is Steal Away to Jesus, sung by Mary Ann Pettway, the current director of the Gee's Bend Quilt Collective in Alabama. Gee's Bend is a small rural community in the bend of the Alabama River south of Selma, famous for its role in the civil rights movement and for the extraordinary quilts the women of Gee's Bend have been producing for over a century. Music has long been at the heart of the community as well, and the quilters sing together as they quilt.

I chose red as the root colour of this song, and let it move to deep pinks and purples. You'll notice that this song is set upon a black canvas. Mary Ann sang freely, stretching phrases or shortening them as she felt the music. This created an uneven length in each line, but a deeply rich texture. Notice also the many trills and ornaments where she embellished the melody. To pay homage to the Gee's Bend style, I hand quilted this piece with an orange peel design and made a scrap-pieced back from fabric remnants from my studio. ❇

elizahardyjones.com
@elizahardyjones

9 ENGLAND 1
45

CHERYL ARKISON

While I quilted before I became a mother, it was motherhood that made me a quilter. That's because I needed to be as honest of a person as I could be to my kids. If I can't be honest with myself, what kind of role model am I for my kids? (Well, that and a year-long mat leave with a kid who really loved to sleep!) That year I accepted my creative passions of quilting and writing, and it changed my life. Now I can't imagine a day without either.

I've written three books: *Sunday Morning Quilts* (co-authored with Amanda Jean Nyberg), *A Month of Sundays* and *You Inspire Me to Quilt*. I've also contributed to numerous other books, magazines and websites as a freelance writer.

One of my absolute favourite things is teaching. I travel nationally and internationally to teach quilting. It is a truly special thing to be invited into the space of creation. I love to break down quilt stereotypes and help people embrace a spirit of adventure with their quilting. I always tell my students that I am here to push them off a cliff, but that I will hold their hand the whole way.

My kids are older now, in school and busy with their chosen extracurriculars. My husband and I also have a small business. My work gets done in the margins of the day. Thank goodness for tea in the morning, scotch at night and cookies all the time.

"I don't like to be just one thing. I want to try things, play and do as much as I feel like doing."

What is your personal relationship or history with quilts? What draws you to them? What led you to the world of quilts?

I've known how to sew from a young age—my mom would make some clothes or sew as a hobby herself. Which meant I always loved looking at fabric and felt comfortable around a sewing machine. I even won the home ec award in Grade 8!

Ultimately, though, it was the fabric that brought me to quilting. In my early 20s, I would walk by a local quilting store and go in to look at the fabric. My boyfriend would roll his eyes but humour me. That being said, I never bought anything because I thought, who makes quilts at 23?! Then his sister announced she was pregnant. "Aha!" I thought, "No one can fault me for making a baby quilt." So I tuned up my mom's old sewing machine, and carried it on the train to the store for a weekend of classes. I was totally hooked from that point on!

From the get-go it was about process more than finished product. Especially as a beginner, you have to really pay attention to what you are doing or you can hurt yourself. Which meant the rest of the world falls away as you make. You are completely present. At the beginning it was stress relief from grad school, now it is sanity-saving as a mom and business owner.

How would you describe your style or aesthetic?

If anything, you could say I have a more-is-more approach to quilting. Why use one white when you could use 10? Why use a solid piece of fabric when you could make fabric from smaller chunks instead? This meshes well with my love for scraps and a scrappy look (they are not the same thing!).

You could also describe me as modern and improvisational. But the truth is that I don't like to be just one thing. I want to try things, play and do as much as I feel like doing. One day that might be perfectly pieced

stars and the next day a round of improv stripes. One day I dig through all my prints to piece and another day I want nothing but solids. If anything, my style is about a willingness to experiment.

What are your intentions when making a quilt or starting a creative project? What thought processes do you typically go through?

I just want to play. Finishing a quilt is like running a marathon. You can't just show up to the race without training. And there are parts of the training that are a slog, but necessary to actually finish the race. I am the kid that just wants to go to the park and run around. I'm not terribly concerned with finishing a race.

More often than not I start a project because I want to see if an idea I had will work. Are the colours good? Is this how it should go together? Can I actually do this? It might stop at that one moment, that one block. I might get jazzed and keep going. Usually, I just start making and wait to see what it will become. That is, I don't start with a pattern already drawn up or my fabric all chosen and cut. At some point, I decide whether what I am doing will actually become a quilt and then I might make a plan. What size quilt? How many more blocks are needed? How will it be sewn together? Then I make it happen. It might take days, weeks, months, even years to move from the idea I played with to a finished quilt.

MORNING MAKES

Everyone comes to quilting for different reasons. Most of us get hung up on having a perfect finished quilt at the end—with the emphasis on perfect and finished. There is a tremendous amount of guilt that comes when you do not achieve either of these things. Personally, I think that is ridiculous. We're coming to quilting to relieve stress, to embrace creativity; to make something thinking only of perfection and completion invites guilt. That is the exact opposite response our quiltmaking should have. That's why I am all about the process.

A few years ago I started a daily practice that I call Morning Make. It comes from the notion of creating before you consume. For me, that means 20 to 60 minutes of silent sewing (or sketching or writing) first thing in the morning. Before the phone, the news, caffeine, and before the kids wake up. It truly has the same benefits as a daily meditation practice because it is all about being present in that moment. It was the smallest change in my sewing habits but it's been life-changing. And now my family knows that we *all* have a better day if I get my Morning Make.

At some point I will push through and finish the quilt, but it's the process that matters. If you only wanted a finished quilt, go to the mall and buy it. I'm in this for the process, not the product.

Have you ever had a quilting or creative failure? What did you learn from it, if anything?

All the time! And you have to learn from it, it's the only way you get better. Then again, what counts as a failure? Getting the time to sew is a win, no matter what happens. Creating is good, even if it doesn't turn out like you expected.

Too many times I've spoken to quilters early in their journey and they lament not being able to make the quilts they want to make—show-quality quilts or complex designs. What everyone needs to remember is that everyone was a beginner once. We only get better by making. You can't play Rachmaninoff on the piano right after you learn Chopsticks. But the more you play and practise, the better you get. With each new project you should learn something, whether it is about colour, value, grain, pressing, seam allowances, binding techniques, whatever.

What quilt traditions do you hold dear? What quilting conventions do you ignore or challenge?

Even though the bulk of my work is improvisational I still believe that you should respect a quarter-inch seam allowance, press your seams and—at some point—square up your work. If your goal is a finished quilt then these things will ensure your finished product lays flat and stays together. After that, pretty much anything goes!

Oh, and I am a big fan of square quilts. There is a part of the quilting world, however, that hates square quilts—I think it comes from bed quilts not being square at all—but I love them in all sizes.

In your opinion or experience, how does the act of quilting bridge the past, present and future?

One of my least favourite expressions is "not your grandmother's quilting." It is generally used whenever someone is under the age of 50 or someone makes something different than a quilt that looks like it belongs in Green Gables. So I don't know if I like thinking of it as a bridge. No one ever asks that about painting or collage or sculpture, do they? It is an art, a craft, a skill that people have been doing for generations, that's it. And like all things, it evolves in technique, design, materials and trends.

I am trying to pass my passion on to my kids. Some days they are into it and some days not so much. I've seen them approach various projects with their own personalities. That fact alone has made me a better teacher—not everyone approaches a challenge the same way and different things challenge different people—and made me a better mother.

Would you consider yourself as a professional within the quilting industry? When and how did you become a professional?

After a major knee injury and two kids, I did a lot of soul searching. I was working on environmental policy and climate change issues and it was a particularly rough time for that. At the same time, my husband's business was growing and he was travelling a lot. I needed a change and we were looking at additional childcare options so I quit my office job. My first week at home coincided with starting my first book in the fall of 2010.

Since then I've evolved my freelance writing career. Two more books and another kid. Now I travel both nationally and internationally to teach quilting. Just don't ask me to pick between writing and teaching, I *love* them both.

What breadth of activity and responsibilities do you have as a professional quilter? Are you able to support yourself in the quilt industry or do you have other endeavours as well?

There are a lot of activities to choose to try and make a living in this game. Almost no one does just one thing. I tried my hand at patterns but it never felt like me because I value improvisation and process over results. I designed a fabric collection with Connecting Threads. It was a great experience and the creative challenge I needed at the time. It is the writing and the teaching that I love the most. Books, articles and even my teenaged blog all still excite me. Teaching, whether online or in person, is exhilarating and inspiring.

A lot of people support themselves in this industry; it is possible. Like any other entrepreneurial endeavour, it takes a strong commitment and a lot of work. We have a family business that pays the bills, and it isn't quilting. But I'm also not in this game for fun. I can always quilt, but if I want to be a professional, anything I commit to outside of family and fun has to be worth the investment.

WORKSPACE

I am lucky to have a bright room in our basement for sewing. I do have to give it up when we have company, but our guests all assure me that they love to stay there among the creativity! It beats the dining room table, where I sewed for 15 years!

In addition to the flip-out sofa bed, the room has a free-standing kitchen island, used as a cutting table and for scraps storage. I do most of my sewing on a repurposed dining table.

My stash is behind closet doors. Some people like to look at their fabric. To me, that is more of a distraction from the work under the needle at the moment. Having two closets to store my stash and my 50-something quilts under construction keeps me focused.

My favourite feature is the design wall. Eight foot square and covered with quilt batting, it allows me to place blocks or components up to play with. As most of my work is designed on the fly, the wall is a necessary tool.

cherylarkison.com
@cheryl_arkison

Too many people short-change themselves in this industry—whether it is selling a finished quilt for less than the true value or accepting free fabric for exposure or not demanding fair terms when they teach. Obviously it isn't exclusive to quilting, but it is pervasive here—enough so that the unfair ask is still always there because someone is willing to accept those terms.

For me, the investment also includes my time, because teaching, for example, takes me away from home and my obligations here. I love it, though, so we make it work. Sure, I could do more and then maybe we could have a nice vacation one day or renovate our gross bathroom, but then I would miss a competition, a performance, making payroll for our employees or simply sitting down to Sunday dinner together.

What motivates and inspires you?

After 21 years I'm still not bored. At one point it was the fabric and colour combinations that got me going. It's easy to get sucked into the newness of fabric when the industry churns out a lot of content twice a year. Now it is the ideas. I have sketchbooks, a whole shelf full, of ideas for quilts. Shape, colour, a mood, a location, an object can all inspire an idea. Then other times I just want to sew fabric together and I have no plan. Actually, I do that a lot.

And the more I do this the more I see and feel the mental health benefits of quiltmaking. So even though my family is buried in quilts, I don't stop making. It's the process, not the product that matters to me. ✻

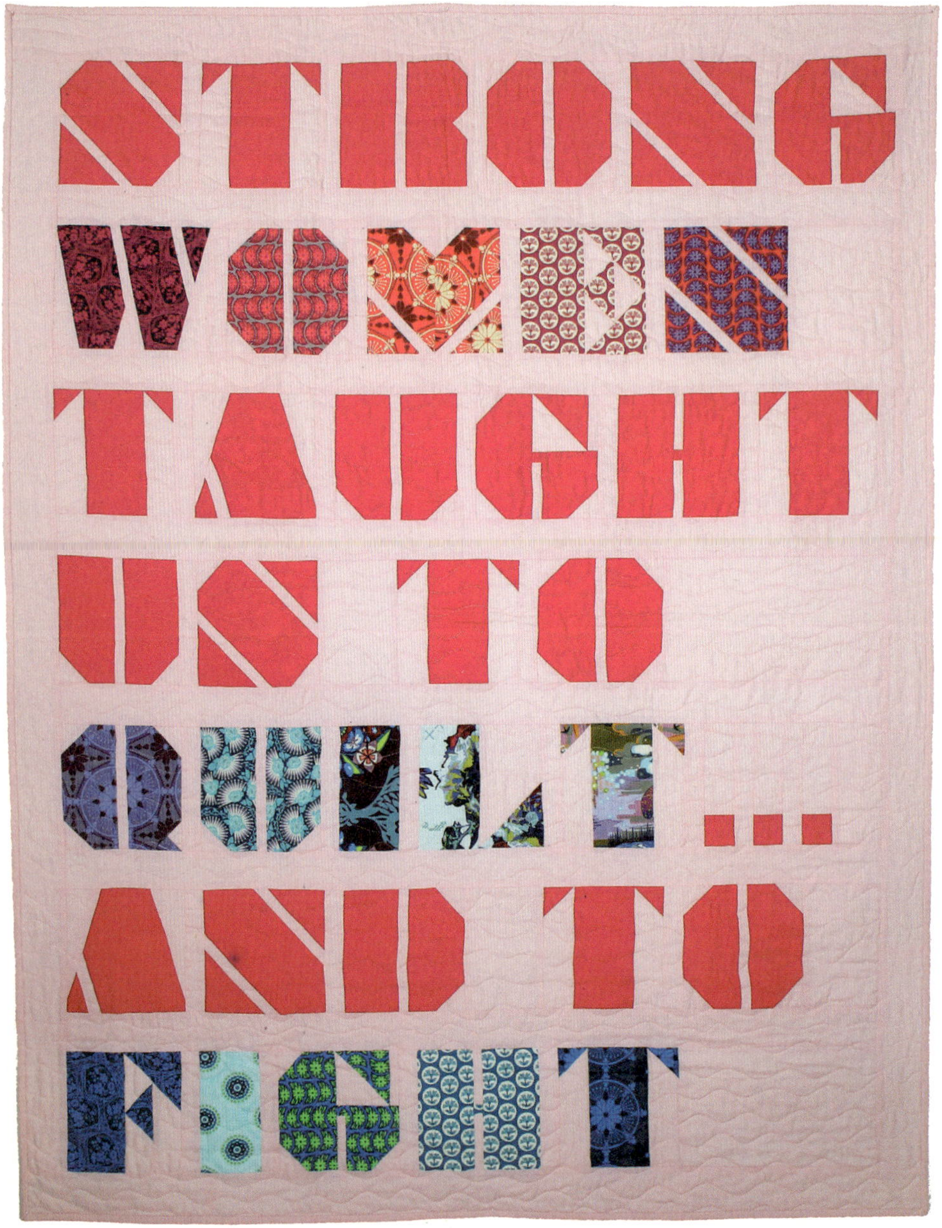
STRONG
WOMEN
TAUGHT
US TO
QUILT...
AND TO
FIGHT

Strong Women

by **Emily Robbins** and **Allison Chambers**

@project.light_emily
@downtownquilter_allie

As the political landscape turned away from values we hold as foundational and fundamental, we knew we wanted to do what so many women had done before us: we chose to add our voices to the protest. Creating quilts as a call to action is nothing new. Women, who were confined to their sphere of domesticity, used their domestic tasks in subversive and powerful ways, creating quilts that reflected their views on politics or other social issues. We wanted to honour the women who taught us to quilt and to fight, and especially those who have used quilting to fight against injustices.

Both of us grew up in a tradition of quilting. We each have formative memories of our grandmothers hand quilting, gathered in circles of women, creating and communing. This was the essential core of our project—no matter what shape it was to take, each step would be done together. We purposely designed letters that stayed true to our overall aesthetic and allowed us to piece them, thereby keeping within the custom of traditional pieced quilts, and we insisted that each stitch was done together. We sewed this quilt side by side in homage to the tradition of women gathering to quilt and commune together while helping one another.

The quilt was first displayed at QuiltCon 2018 and it resonated with viewers, who shared it through their social media, commented on our Instagram posts and reached out in private messages. At least one quilter even got the quilt's message tattooed on her leg!

Our quilt has done what we hoped it would: remind our community that women have been collaborating, communing, quilting, protesting and enacting change for centuries. We are so thankful to be a part of this beautiful and strong tradition. ❇

CHRIS ENGLISH

I live in Huddersfield in West Yorkshire, United Kingdom. I have a teenage son, Bailey, who lives with me for part of the week. I work in e-commerce and I quilt as a hobby and as a way to stay creative. I've always loved art and design, and studied textile design at the University of Liverpool many years ago. Since then I'd always done different creative classes but nothing really stuck until I discovered quilting. I found a simple brick pattern in a Liberty home sewing book and was able to make it. This also coincided with there being a local quilt shop in Huddersfield where I was able to take a couple of classes with some amazing quilters—Luke Haynes and Sarah Fielke probably being the biggest influences. I've started quilting more since I stopped playing football (soccer) and found that when I wasn't doing anything I was becoming frustrated and realized that I definitely needed a way to express myself, especially after a tough day at work.

What is your personal relationship or history with quilts? What draws you to them? What led you to the world of quilts?

I remember screen printing fabric at high school and making a very basic pair of board shorts! I studied art and design at college and went on to study textile design in university. I loved my time there—drawing and painting all day was fantastic—but reality hit home when I left and I couldn't get a job in that industry.

I retained an interest in print and fabric design, and found that quilting was the natural outlet for my creativity. I'm particularly drawn to improvisational quilts and those that are made out of necessity. I love the Gee's Bend quilts and how the quiltmakers there used whatever fabric was available to them.

How would you describe your style or aesthetic?

My style is modern, improvisational, punky and practical, by which I mean I combine a mixture of blocks with improvisational piecing techniques. I love using recycled fabric and this can often influence the direction my quilts take.

However, I do absolutely love traditional quilts (I fell in love with Baltimore Album quilts after seeing an exhibition at this year's Festival of Quilts), and whilst I'm probably never going to make one they do directly influence my work.

The practical element of my approach refers to the fact that my quilts are made to be used as quilts, and to my approach of sourcing fabric. I like to use what I have and what I can find. I do occasionally buy new fabric but these days that is pretty rare.

I use a mix of traditional techniques and an improv approach, and in particular I use a strip-piecing approach where I'll join scraps to strips of fabric and effectively create a large piece of fabric that I'll cut up again and sew back together. I find that this approach creates really interesting patterns and juxtapositions of pattern that you wouldn't be able to plan.

The punk influence is about that approach, if you can play three chords you can make a punk record. I kind of think that if you can sew a straight line you can make an improv quilt. I think quilt making is accessible to everyone.

What are your intentions when making a quilt or starting a creative project? What thought processes do you typically go through?

I experiment with different ideas and processes, and these small initial experiments often evolve into a full-size quilt. Because I use predominantly found and recycled fabric I often find that this will suggest an approach or a colour combination that I want to explore.

Often I know that I'm making a quilt for a specific person or for an exhibition, so I'll use colour, fabric and imagery that I think the recipient will like.

What mindset or attitude do you think is best for quilting? How does quilting affect your mental and physical health?

Quilting is a creative release for me. I believe that everyone is creative and that it's really important to be able to express yourself creatively and find an outlet for it. I find that different parts of the process are good for different things, sitting and sewing a binding on can be very relaxing and ultimately satisfying as you finish a quilt. Sometimes, though, I'll have a burst of creative energy and that's when I like to choose colours and fabrics, and be improvisational. I find that when I feel like this I make braver and more exciting choices. Equally, I find reading about quilts or listening to podcasts a relaxing part of the process, and don't beat myself up if I don't feel like sewing.

I find creating crumb blocks (sewing scraps together in an improv way) is really relaxing and I'll often empty a bag of scraps and just sew with no plan in mind and just see what happens. There's definitely satisfaction in working through the massive pile of scraps I have, knowing that eventually they'll become a useful quilt.

I love gifting my quilts as well, and giving something handmade to somebody is a great feeling. For secret Santa at work now I always make a cushion for whomever I draw—and so far people have loved it, much better than buying something they don't want and that will likely end up in the bin.

"If you're unsure about starting a quilt then I'd absolutely say go for it. Quilts don't need to be perfect or use expensive fabric, often the more simple quilts turn out the most beautiful. Once you've made the quilt, get it on the bed in winter and turn the heating down a bit and help save the planet."

"I don't worry about failing and have kind of accepted it as part of the creative process."

Have you ever had a quilting or creative failure? What happened? What did you learn from it, if anything?

Yep, all of the time. Part of my creative process and quilting process is to fail and to learn from those failures. It might be something technical that fails and that's usually quite easy to fix, whereas if it's something more creative such as colour or fabric choice then that can be a bit more challenging. But if I don't like it I tend to cut it up and sew it back together until I do like it.

I always have a small A5-size sketchbook and this gets filled with sketches and stuff I find. It can often be the juxtaposition of these that will spark the idea for a quilt, so I'll often know what I'm setting out to do. However, this will often change and evolve as I create.

I do have a pile of sample pieces that I keep as a reference and will sometimes use as part of a swap or as a small gift.

What quilt traditions do you hold dear? What quilting conventions do you ignore or challenge?

The most important quilting tradition for me is that quilts should be practical and be used. Another thing is to use the fabric you have on hand. Although I occasionally buy new fabric, my favourite source is my local flea market or charity shops, where I can get a lot of fabric at really good value. It also encourages me to make bolder fabric choices, as I'm not spending loads of money and worrying about ruining the fabric.

I don't worry too much about stuff like stitch length—hand quilting has quite a relaxed approach. I like my quilting to be seen so I like to use big stitches. I definitely don't mind if they aren't perfect.

I'm not too worried if my points match and I suppose my style means that these things aren't hugely important, and if there is something I don't like then I'll appliqué something over the piece I don't like.

I don't follow any rules when it comes to colour usage and I'm happy to go with my instinct for what feels right at the time. The same goes for using prints, and I love mixing prints, florals and stripes all together to create an overall effect.

In your opinion or experience, how does the act of quilting bridge the past, present and future?

Quilting absolutely bridges time and generations. I use fabric in my quilts from my old worn-out work clothes and I've got a quilt that has shirt fabric from my interview for my first job (over 20 years ago). Hopefully, this quilt will long outlive me.

I'm interested in how the found fabric I use has had a former life as a garment and will now have a future life as a quilt and become a practical and treasured family heirloom.

I like to rescue quilts from charity shops and auctions and use them at home. I'm interested in the history of these quilts and love that someone has taken the time to create them. I wish more had labels so I could understand where they came from. It's great as well to give these quilts a new purpose, and that they become part of my traditions.

My son, Bailey, also gets a quilt each year instead of a PS4 game. He moans now but I'm convinced that one day these quilts will be something that he loves and that he'll use with his family. Often these quilts will contain some of his old clothes or bedding, and act as a bridge between the past and the future.

Do any particular ideas, objects or activities—outside of and unrelated to quilting—inform and inspire your quilting practice?

Loads of stuff from outside of quilting influences me. I collect fat lava ceramics, vintage advertising, stamps and anything else that I find visually interesting. I've got loads of sketchbooks where I keep all this material and use it as a reference.

I was massively influenced as well by the recent Extinction Rebellion protest about climate change in Leeds. I really felt that this is an important thing to speak up about and do something about. ❇

INSPIRATION

I'm inspired by lots of things. A big influence is travel and I love visiting big cities. New York is my favourite city and I love the energy it has. I take loads of pictures of the street art and this definitely has impacted my quilting, especially my hand quilting and appliqué. I love the juxtaposition of different street artists' work and how over time layers and textures develop, and I try to recreate this with my use of loads of different fabric and quilting. I'll mix machine quilting, hand quilting and appliqué to generate this effect.

WORKSPACE

I sew at home, and whilst I don't have a dedicated sewing space, I do have a big space, so when I'm working on a project I can spread out and trial layouts and ideas as I go. This is important for me, as my style is improvisational. I love that my space is at home, as I can sew when I want and I've got examples of all the stuff that influences me around me. I'm a very visual person so having things to look at and refer to helps to inspire me. I probably need to better separate the space in my house and try to stop quilting projects taking over everywhere.

chrisenglishquilts.com
@afullenglish

DENYSE SCHMIDT

I'm a designer-maker with an interest in history and a predilection for patina. I seem to have a highly developed, innate attention to detail—I am always noticing things that others don't see. I have respect for craft, and am mostly interested in making functional, well-designed and beautiful objects. I'm an initiator—I don't always have the patience to see things through to the bitter end—so it's interesting that I chose quilts, and that I haven't gotten bored with making them. The medium still holds so much potential and inspiration for me.

I grew up in central Massachusetts in the 1960s and 1970s, the youngest of four kids. My parents were skilled makers of practical things they made out of need and thriftiness. Nothing they made ever felt homemade, and I took it for granted that this was how everyone lived. New England is filled with towns like mine—built around old brick mills, most of them having formerly produced textiles. I always say that this landscape really informed the "fabric" of who I am today—it's really true! I was always making things—dolls, softies, all kinds of stuff—and inventing worlds like most kids.

After a few twists and turns, I eventually went to art school (Rhode Island School of Design) and studied graphic design. It served me well at that time of big changes in the industry, but when my first permanent job felt stifling, I jumped ship and decided to make quilts for a living! It sounds crazy now, but my understanding boss and decent pay enabled me to slowly transition to working part time, and that made it possible for me to build the business without a lot of pressure or debt.

"I feel that quilting is and has always been so approachable. Anyone can do it, and good work can be made at any skill level."

"I love the idea of intentionally including a mistake block in a quilt. For the Amish I believe it represents their humbleness, as only God can make something perfect. I adhere to the idea that *if* a mistake happens, by all means include it, but don't go imposing accidents."

What is your personal relationship or history with quilts? What draws you to them? What led you to the world of quilts?

Some years after I started my business, my mother told me that someone in our family—her grandmother possibly—made what we would call "utilitarian" quilts (quickly stitched together out of upcycled clothing or other textiles for immediate, regular use). None of the quilts survived (as is typical), and though my mother sewed clothing for herself and us four kids, she never made a quilt. The closest I ever got to a quilt growing up was a brown/orange/gold cheater cloth bedcover that was quilted with synthetic thread, probably from Sears.

When I graduated from art school in 1982, I moved to Connecticut for a guy I barely knew. The relationship slowly revealed itself as a bad idea over the course of a few years, and in the interim I felt particularly disconnected from my tribe in those pre-Internet days. I was exposed to old-time music through the fiddle-playing boyfriend. I was fascinated with this seemingly wholesome subculture of string band

music and contra dancing that I absorbed through recordings that documented the scratchy, repetitive folk music of the 1920s and 1930s, and how the same tune evolved in distinctly different ways by region. I romanticized the era through the filter of sepia-toned WPA photographs and old films depicting folks playing, rolling up the rug for a Friday night dance, wearing their feedsack dresses and especially helping each other out with barn raisings and quilting bees. In retrospect, I believe this idea of life in a supportive, connected community at a time when I was feeling isolated had a strong impact. At the same time, Martha Stewart was reinventing the genre of women's magazines and presenting traditional domestic arts in a beautiful, sophisticated style that felt fresh and new. These influences and probably an overreaction to the ephemeral nature and mass-market aesthetics of the graphic design work I was doing at the time all conspired to bring my attention to this age-old craft.

What are your intentions when making a quilt or starting a creative project? What thought processes do you typically go through?

It really depends on the project. For instance, designing a pattern to showcase a fabric range takes a different mindset than creating a series of one-off quilts that are for an exhibition. But almost all creative projects require a sort of clean slate—tidying up the studio is a way to reset my brain. In very general terms, all projects begin with a gathering of information and inspiration. This may happen subconsciously over time, as well as purposefully as I prepare more physically for working on the project. Designing quilt patterns and fabrics for home sewers involves very specific parameters and constraints (which is a very satisfying process for me), and the intentions are clear and fairly obvious. Designing for myself—creating work that doesn't need to be duplicated or doesn't need easily written and translated instructions—is more challenging. I will impose parameters—sometimes arbitrary—to limit the variables, as otherwise it's too wide open for me to wrap my brain around. The intention is usually to challenge myself—to explore some idea I've been mulling over for some time, to use some particular fabrics—and always to make something beautiful. Like all creative people, I can get stuck and go through periods of self-doubt, so always going back to the limits and intentions is helpful.

ON FAILURES

Most of the failures I have conveniently forgotten, but one I remember was when I worked with a women's cooperative in New Mexico to launch a more affordable printed bedding and tabletop line. I didn't have a lot of money (luckily), so all the mistakes and assumptions I made didn't take as big of a toll as they could have. Almost every item I designed had its own screen—an upfront investment that no one with more experience would have made. I assumed the audience I had established over the preceding few years would overlap more than it actually did with the audience for this new product—you have to have a much wider distribution for things with low margins made in quantity, and it takes time to build those channels of distribution and grow the audience. The many lessons I learned from this endeavour were invaluable, and prevented me from making many more potentially worse errors in the coming years.

When and how did you become a professional?

I began making finished quilts for a living in 1996, and around 2005 or so I started designing fabric for the industry-end of quilting, as most of us know it.

What breadth of activity and responsibilities do you have as a professional quilter?

Our current environment of low-cost digital everything—where social media is how you market yourself, and anyone can put up a website and sell from it—has made it possible for anyone to establish a business and be able to successfully operate with very little overhead. It was very different when I began my business in 1996, when everything was expensive and had to be outsourced, and the only way to reach an audience was through advertising, or mail campaigns! So I have evolved from working on my own, through having employees, and back around to working mostly alone again—and doing *all of it*. Managing people is not my strong point, and I love the freedom of being on my own.

What motivates and inspires you?

Deadlines are the most reliable motivators, as I can enjoy the designing, thinking, dreaming stage forever! I'm inspired by many things, including artists who work year after year with a disciplined and narrow focus, the accidental juxtapositions of things, happenstance, folk art, vernacular typography and signage, the work of self-taught artists, Shaker architecture and craft, colonial-era weaving and craft, and nature.

Do any particular ideas, objects or activities—outside of and unrelated to quilting—inform and inspire your quilting practice?

My garden and working in my garden, films, music, being in nature.

"My style is rooted in tradition, with a current sensibility informed by my eclectic interests, experiences and point of view."

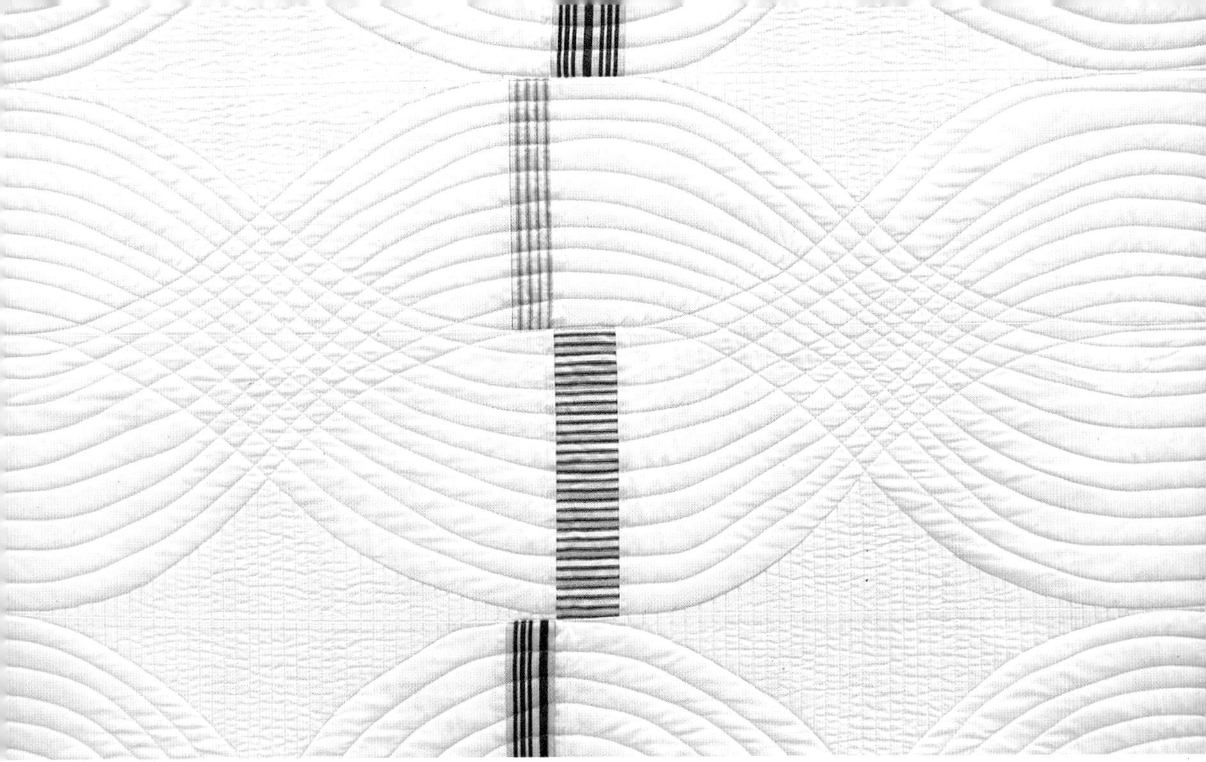

In your opinion or experience, how does the act of quilting bridge the past, present and future?

Quilting is a uniquely American traditional art form that has the ability to bind the past to the present and the future. A quilt can become a family heirloom by sewing together favourite old fabrics and pieces of clothing that hold special significance to create a family history. A quilt that includes a piece of your granny's favourite dress or your dad's tie provides emotional coziness and a sense of continuity, and sparks memories that add far more value than simply physical warmth! The act of patchwork quilting is also a lovely metaphor for America itself—the coming together of the seemingly disparate to create a whole new entity—one made stronger and more colourful for its diversity. ❇

WORKSPACE

I have a 1,100-square-foot studio on the 4th floor of a 1000 ioh footory building whoro lace trims were manufactured, in Bridgeport, Connecticut. The studio has 16-foot ceilings, and south- and west-facing windows. Lots of light! The windows are in bad shape and it's mostly too hot in the summer and too cold in the winter. I have been itching to change up my studio situation, but am struggling to figure out what it will be. After 15-plus years, I'm tired of the dirt that rains down from the wood ceiling and that makes its way in from the windows, and I'd like to be able to easily run out for a coffee or lunch. I sew on a 35-year-old Brother industrial straight stitch. I also do some work out of my home (a 10-minute drive) when I am able, including bookkeeping, writing and handwork.

dsquilts.com
@dsquilts

M-Lisada Orphanage Kampala, Uganda

by **Ellen Ruden**

I volunteer at M-Lisada, an amazing orphanage in Uganda where I started teaching quilting in 2013. After taking Denyse Schmidt's "A Different Stripe" workshop, I knew that her fun and forgiving pattern would be a great way to introduce the kids and staff to improvisational quilting. Denyse graciously let me bypass the design copyright, since all the sales from these quilts are donated directly to M-Lisada.

This quilt was our first improv attempt in my February 2018 class—they loved learning this new technique. It was gifted to my dear friend, Leonard, who generously funded my second volunteer trip in 2016. We completed five large quilts while I was there, and since then, returning volunteers continue to bring me more finished quilts. I'm selling them at home in the United States, and every penny helps M-Lisada provide food, clean water, education and healthcare.

"We bonded and formed lifelong friendships like I imagine has happened at every quilting bee for centuries."

We had so much fun creating these colourful works of art. We talked and laughed and sang and shared ideas and the workload. Their faces lit up with each reveal of new notions or pretty fabric. We bonded and formed lifelong friendships like I imagine has happened at every quilting bee for centuries. I loved watching their skills and confidence grow during those two weeks and it has been exciting to see the different layouts they've been designing since I left. I could not be more proud of my talented, hardworking students!

Before each trip, I collect fabric donations. The quilting community on Instagram blew me away by supplying six full suitcases for my improv classes, with lots of extra material so that students can continue making quilts to generate income.

I have met some of the most incredible people at M-Lisada and a piece of my heart will always belong to Uganda. ✻

ellengracequilts.com
@ellengracequilts

DIANA FOX-REVETT

In my journey as an artist, I have always been drawn to textiles. Whether through dyeing, printing, sewing, knitting or embroidery, there is something about the physicality of working with fabric, the touch and feel of cloth and the act of a needle passing through them that I cannot resist. For me the pursuit of mastery of various techniques, while in service of expressing my creative vision, is immensely rewarding. After graduating in surface design from OCAD in Toronto, followed by a stint studying textiles and art history at NSCAD in Halifax, I spent two decades as a colourist and designer in the wall covering industry. While my own work had to take a back seat, recently I have been able to devote myself to being a full-time artist.

Today my mind is always swirling with new ideas and most of the time it starts with fabric. It would be unusual to see me without work in my hands. It goes everywhere with me, and I find a thousand different occasions to pull a small piece from my bag. In this way, the finished piece has travelled my path and witnessed the world I inhabit.

"Quilting synthesizes all my creative passions: design, colour, fabric and stitching. It has a long pedigree of tradition that is firmly rooted in purpose. Quilts are in equal measures practical and whimsical, beautiful and functional."

How would you describe your style or aesthetic?

My quilts are modern and are unabashedly dominated by my passion for colour. My style tends to be clean and graphic, but I use relaxed organic lines and often circular shapes. Improvisation is at the very heart of my process. Nothing is predetermined or planned out. Typically, I will start with an idea of a colour palette that I want to explore, or perhaps a specific technique

ANDREW EDDY

that I want to play with. Then I'll dive headlong into it, cutting fabric and sewing pieces together to see where this leads me. I may put a section together only to later cut it up and rearrange it.

I will start small and then as I immerse myself in the process I will continue to build up the piece, choosing colours in response to what is emerging at each stage, and accept that along this winding path it may morph into something else entirely. It's not random, but nor is it planned out in advance. I am especially drawn to organic lines and circles, and I use them frequently in my work as well as search them out in the natural world. Lately, I have been hand piecing my quilt tops and then hand quilting the layers together.

What are your intentions when making a quilt or starting a creative project? What thought processes do you typically go through?

I find the greatest inspiration and satisfaction in the process of experimentation. The simple act of making is intrinsically rewarding and calming. It gives me peace of mind when everything else in the world can seem out of control. In many ways, this is an end unto itself and I am grateful for it as a stabilizing influence in my life.

But once I'm immersed in it, the motivation comes to me in different forms, without necessarily having fully contemplated an idea for the overall piece. Certainly, I'm not executing a predetermined concept and don't have final dimensions in mind. The output is revealed only over time.

Colour combinations and fabric choices excite me at the moment. Keeping a pile of fabric scraps at the ready is important. Putting colours and patterns next to one another to see their effect upon each other is constantly stimulating. I am invested in continuing on the project to see where it leads, and in the next moment excited by a new idea or colour story that is sparked by that work. Sometimes a small element catalyzes an idea for my project. My work tends to be slow and allows for lots of meandering and my natural curiosity, and often I have several projects on the go at the same time.

What mindset or attitude do you think is best for quilting? How does quilting affect your mental and physical health?

If I bring one thing to my quilting, it is a sense of play. And I hope that this infuses my work with joy and happiness. If it solicits a reaction from people along those lines then I consider my work successful.

You might consider this out of step with the utilitarian origins of the quilt, but then consider that quilting was the kind of activity done at the end of a long day, sometimes a solitary effort after other work was done, or sometimes socially when quilters would gather. Even today, sharing my work as part of my local quilt guild or just striking up a conversation with

someone who sees me sewing in the coffee shop encourages me to keep moving forward. Play takes me down a path of continual experimentation with various combinations of colour and solids versus printed fabrics. Improvisation allows me to be playfully in the moment and to enjoy the process no matter how irregular and nonlinear.

Have you ever had a quilting or creative failure? What happened? What did you learn from it, if anything?

I would challenge the notion of failures. Rather, each piece and each stitch within it is part of my journey. This isn't to say that learning a new technique, like English paper piecing, doesn't require practice—it does. When I look back at my work, I can see the connections. I can see how one thing has led to another and how an earlier effort echoes and builds within the next piece.

When I don't like something—what others might consider failure—I rework it. I cut it up. Maybe even put it aside. And this is perhaps where the fundamental difference in my process is most evident. Traditional quilting builds on a foundation of patterns and layouts, of working in block patterns and multiples; it follows a linear path. Giving yourself license to diverge, to branch out in a new direction or to run with something even if it leads to a dead-end is what pleases me most about my approach.

I am trying to finish up some quilt tops that I started working on several years ago. I confess that I'm finding it difficult to go back and continue those pieces. I love them but my work feels different to me now and going back isn't always easy. Accepting that not all work needs to be finished has been a hard lesson. Perhaps we need to give ourselves permission to move on, knowing it will inform our future work.

What quilt traditions do you hold dear? What quilting conventions do you ignore or challenge?

My own quilted work is rooted in the simplest tradition of putting two smaller pieces of fabric together, but from that starting point, I seek to liberate myself to explore the merging of shapes and colours. As I work, the tradition and history of the process rattles around in my brain, but otherwise I am unencumbered by convention.

In my improv quilt work, I do not use sashing between blocks; in fact, I rarely work in a block format at all. Instead, I make irregular shapes that I sew together with other irregular shapes and build my quilt almost as a puzzle. A ruler is of little use to me, as I prefer irregular organic lines and work without final dimensions in mind.

If there is a tradition that I aspire to, it is in the quality of the finished work. I want my work to be the best I can make it. Deliberate and delicate stitching. And when marrying the pieced top with the backing, I consider how quilting, either by machine or more often by hand, can cohesively transform the finished piece.

"Even when I'm not quilting, I find I'm reacting to colour combinations all around me. The bright greens of fresh spring. The blues of the lake and mountains. Both in my daily routine or when I venture out in search of them, I'm constantly observing."

In your opinion or experience, how does the act of quilting bridge the past, present and future?

There is something intrinsically enduring about quilting. Perhaps this is because of its legacy as a practical

WORKSPACE

My studio space at Artscape Youngplace in Toronto is home base for me. It's a renovated classroom with high ceilings and tall windows. The chalkboard on one wall is both a message board and home for clippings and photos. It's where I have my sewing machine and piles of fabric scraps. When a piece is nearly done, this is where it seems to come together and where I can stand back and see the whole piece. There are opportunities here for impromptu feedback. It's a place separate from the everyday where I can put something down and then pick it up where I left off.

The studio is a perfect complement to my hand sewing, which is so portable that I can work anywhere—at home on my dining table with my family around, in coffee shops, public libraries, airplanes while travelling... literally anywhere.

solution to the need for comfort and warmth. They originated in a time when things were still made by hand, and perfectly good fabric pieces were too valuable not to find another life for them. Quilters today keep alive the craftsmanship and techniques of their predecessors while bringing their own aesthetics and a fresh sense of design. Quilts, as a medium for artistic expression, are still anchored in their heritage as objects.

At the same time, there is something temporal about the quilt, particularly when it is put to use. The puckering around the stitches after washing, the fading of fabric, the odd rip or stain—quilts bear witness to a life of usefulness. In the history of the scraps that go into making them, to the hours spent sewing them, to the lives they share when done and the memories they will embody as they pass among generations—they exist and have a purpose in the past, present and future. Through sewing, I feel connected to the generations of women who have made domestic things through the centuries.

What motivates and inspires you?

The constant exploration of colour relationships continues to motivate me. My response to the positioning of different fabric patterns and colours is immediate and instinctive. Something excites me about these revelations and it urges me to keep going. The process is absorbing for me and I can easily lose track of time. ❄

"There is an investment of time that is required to complete a quilt. In the act of their making, there are quiet moments of focus that inspire meditation and reflection. I find comfort in the elemental aspects of the process. But this is punctuated with moments of playfulness and surprise that come from improvisation and a hunger to explore the merging of shapes and colours."

@pinkinked

DIANE MELMS

Working in cloth was a tradition in my family and my mother taught me to sew when I was about 10 years old. She started me with simple handwork but eventually I was making most of my own clothes. I was also always passionate about art. As a child, I would slip away to my bedroom and draw and paint for hours. In school, I used art to express myself in all areas of study. I majored in art in college and loved learning about all forms of art. After college, I moved to Alaska, married, raised a family and enjoyed a long and fulfilling career teaching art in public schools. Learning about art, teaching art and making art has been a lifelong pursuit.

The work I am doing now is the perfect combination of my skills and passions. Making art with fabric using my sewing skills and my art and design background is very gratifying. I make contemporary quilts using an improvisational approach to creating my own original designs. I love creating art with cloth and stitch. I find the process suits me. I delight in the tactile experience of working with cloth, and I find the tools and techniques available offer a wide range of possibilities for expressing my ideas. My fabric compositions are complex examples of contemporary art, made to hang on the wall like a painting.

What is your personal relationship or history with quilts? What draws you to them? What led you to the world of quilts?

I have a heartfelt appreciation for quilts and their makers. I cherish the hand-sewn quilts that were passed down from my mother and grandmother, I marvel at their craftsmanship and perseverance.

"I aspire to connect with other people through my art, creating work that is visually compelling, technically interesting and psychologically uplifting."

DIANE MELMS, ZACHARY MELMS, CHRIS AREND

"I consider the use of design elements and the application of design principles from the very beginning of an idea. Because I create mostly nonrepresentational images, I strive to express my ideas using colour, line, shape, pattern and the configuration of those elements. My goal is to effectively use the expressive power of abstract design to communicate feelings or ideas."

When I hold these treasured objects, I can feel their presence and their love.

I became interested in making quilts myself when a group of friends invited me to join their quilting group. I loved the sewing and working with fabrics, but making quilts using patterns did not suit me. I wanted to do it my way! I was a renegade.

I was introduced to making "quilts as art" when I discovered the work of renowned art quilters Yvonne Porcella and Nancy Crow. Their colourful graphic quilts captivated me. They redefined what a quilt could be. Over the years, I have taken a number of classes from Nancy where I was introduced to a variety of improvisational approaches to creating compositions in cloth. The work was very challenging but I was enthralled with the process. I also took classes from several other acclaimed textile artists and have learned to dye my own fabric, print patterns on cloth and use free-motion stitching to add detailed stitching to my designs. I was determined to build my skills and committed to creating my own original quilt designs.

How would you describe your style or aesthetic?

My quilts are primarily abstract explorations of form and colour, and the emotions evoked by these elements. Colour relationships, patterns, transitions and movement are of utmost

importance to me. My intent is to create engaging compositions that communicate feelings or ideas, create a sense of place or a state of mind, or suggest a kind of movement. My works convey a variety of moods, and might individually be described as flowing, dynamic or playful.

I have explored many different styles and techniques in my quilt making, from finely pieced linear compositions to layered and organic raw-edge appliqué. I tend to work in series and like to take an idea and explore the possibilities. I have created several large bodies of work that represent my exploration of a specific style, theme or technique.

What are your intentions when making a quilt or starting a creative project? What thought processes do you typically go through?

I start each piece with a general idea and will often make several rough sketches. I then consider which construction technique I will use. Geometric designs lend themselves to machine piecing but designs with more organic shapes are best constructed using raw-edge appliqué. Once my idea is clear in my mind, I will select a colour scheme and begin working directly with the fabric, letting the composition evolve on my design wall. I will cut shapes freehand and organize them into different configurations, or sew together small pieced design units that will be arranged and rearranged on the wall to create the desired composition. Consideration of design principles is always in play, as I am constantly analyzing my work in progress, thinking about the colour relationship, and about movement in the piece, creating a focal point or balancing an arrangement. This improvised way of working with design is the most engaging part of the process for me.

What mindset or attitude do you think is best for quilting? How does quilting affect your mental and physical health?

Creating art is a process of discovery. To achieve the goal of creating original quilt art, you must approach it with a growth mindset, focusing on the process rather than the product. You should be willing to take risks, try new ideas and not be afraid to fail. Failure is part of the creative process and having a willingness to work with it and learn from it is critical.

You must also be willing to make the effort, do the work and put in the necessary time. Making quilts is not a fast process. It can be technically challenging, labour intensive and time consuming. Patience and perseverance are necessary characteristics for all quiltmakers, whether you create original designs or make traditional quilts using patterns.

For me, serious studio work demands my full attention. When doing creative problem solving I am deep in thought. It is an activity that I do best in isolation, or at least I need to mentally isolate myself. At home in the studio, when I am in the midst of creating, my husband says it is as if I am on another planet.

Making art is an essential element to my well-being. It stimulates my mind, helps me to deal with anxiety and gives me an outlet for expressing thoughts, feelings and ideas. It gives me joy!

What quilt traditions do you hold dear? What quilting conventions do you ignore or challenge?

I value the tradition of creating quilts from scraps and repurposed fabric, as our ancestors did. The glut of cast-off clothing and textiles in the world is creating an environmental crisis. Repurposed fabric is an honourable and ethical source for quilt materials.

In terms of the quilt itself, I pretty much ignore any of the "quilt police" quality standards practised by judges of traditional quilt competitions. Rules

"Making rushed decisions about composition doesn't pay. When doing a final critique, you need time to consider it carefully from many points of view. Looking at it with fresh eyes the next day is a good idea. Trust your instincts and don't assemble the layers before fully evaluating the composition. If it isn't working, it is worth taking drastic measures to fix it."

about having perfect matching points, consistent seam allowances and even stitching are not important to me. Although I practise good craftsmanship, I do not seek technical perfection in my work, and hold a higher regard for pieces with expressive qualities and strong design.

I also challenge the often-expressed notion that quilting falls into the category of being a craft but not art. Original art made with fabric using the quilt form is unquestionably art in every respect, and worthy of being accepted as such, and displayed in respected galleries alongside other recognized art forms.

In your opinion or experience, how does the act of quilting bridge the past, present and future?

Quilts tell the stories of their time and can carry an innate message from the creators. They are evidence of historic trends, artistic style, skills, effort and time spent. We are connected to the past by collecting historical quilts, preserving them and researching their histories. Through studying the quilt creations of the women who went before us, we honour their creative efforts, learn from them and carry this art form into the future.

Contemporary quilters who use the quilt form to express new ideas are pushing this work into new territory. The quilts made today will tell the stories of our times and be a testament to the fantastically creative quilt artists of the 21st century.

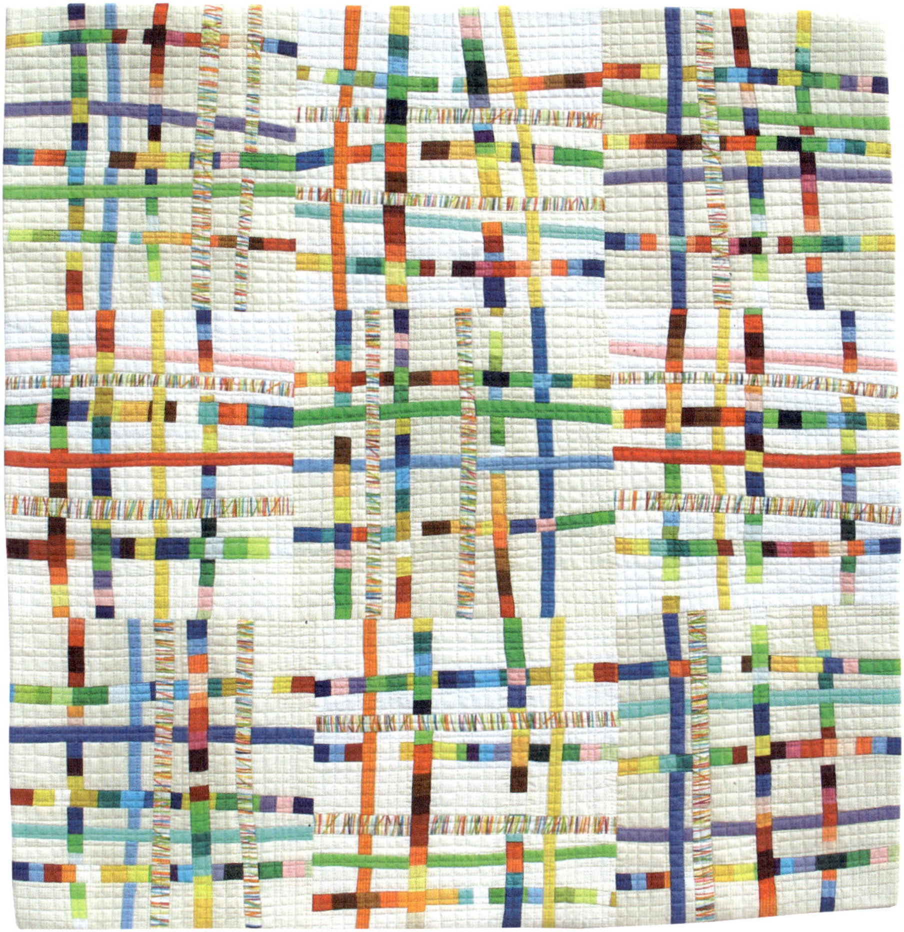

"I have high regard for the practice of making quilts as special gifts for loved ones, babies, brides, veterans, the sick and the underprivileged. Quilts made for someone special are gifts of time and love. The tradition of the quilting bee is also very dear to me, and I very much enjoy being part of a local art quilting network. We gather to share our creations, work on community projects and learn from each other."

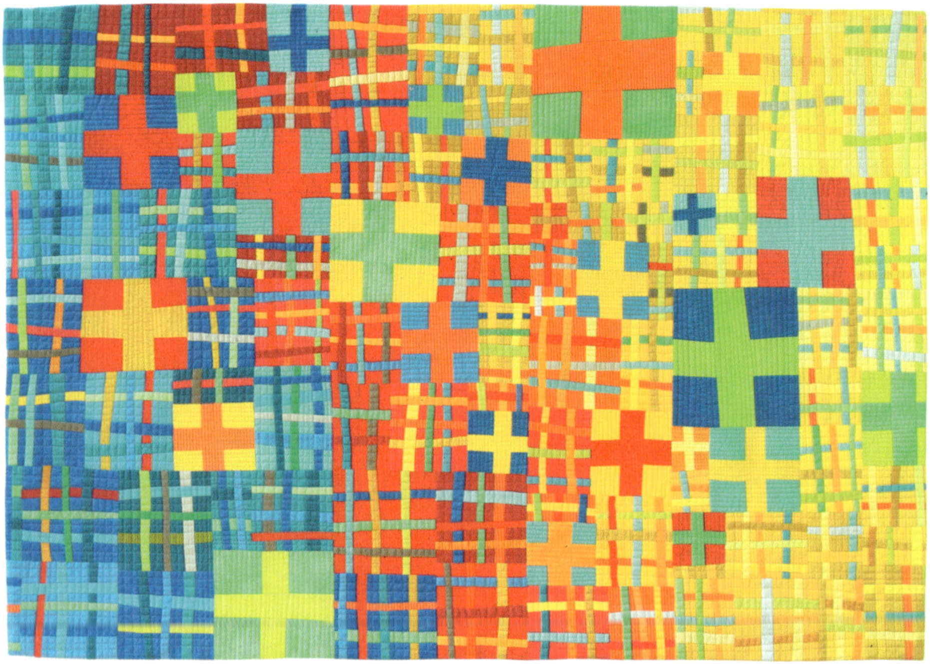

Would you consider yourself a professional?

When I retired from teaching art and decided to become a serious studio artist, I knew it would take considerable time to build the skills, develop my artistic voice and create a cohesive body of work. I had a formal art background, and had explored and taught many different forms of art over the years, but I was lacking a depth of experience in a specific field. I experimented with ideas and techniques, and made lots of art in an effort to find and develop my artistic voice. It took more than five years to create a cohesive body of work that I felt was worthy of exhibition.

I feel like I became a professional quilter when I began showing my work in galleries and entering it into juried art exhibits. The sale of art from my first gallery show was very exciting, but when two pieces were accepted into a prestigious exhibit at the Anchorage Art Museum, and I won the Jurors Award, it confirmed my commitment to becoming a professional quilt artist.

What breadth of activity and responsibilities do you have?

As a professional artist, my primary responsibility is to create new and exciting quilted artwork. I seek out quilt shows, galleries and museums, and submit work to local, national and international juried exhibits. I travel to attend openings when a piece is accepted, prepare artist statements and give artist talks. I have created, compiled, designed and hung three solo exhibits, coordinating the shipping of artwork to venues. I prepare promotional materials (cards, postcards, posters) and maintain my website.

Although my work is available for sale, and pieces do sell from galleries and exhibits, I do not actively market it. It gives me satisfaction to have my work selected for purchase by an appreciative art consumer, but I fall short when it comes to promoting it. I do not depend on income from quilting to sustain me.

What motivates and inspires you?

My greatest motivation is love of the process. I am enamoured with making art with fabric: I love creating colours and patterns using dye or paint, making lines and textures with stamps or stitches, sewing, free-motion quilting, improvisational design work and creative problem-solving. It's all good!

I am also motivated by the challenge of entering work in juried exhibits, and work well with deadlines. The desire to get work into a prestigious exhibit can be a great motivation to create new and exciting work.

I am motivated to create a body of work that is evidence of my artistic vision. It will be my legacy. It will represent my feelings and ideas, my skills and interests, my values and affections. It will embody my spirit. ❇

dianemelms.com
@dianemelmsartist

WORKSPACE

When I retired from teaching we remodelled our garage to create a large studio. I love having a dedicated space where I can walk away from ongoing projects and return with everything still in place. I have a huge worktable, several different kinds of sewing machines, ample cabinets for storage and a variety of portable design walls. My fabric is organized into trays and totes tucked away in cabinets and stored under tables on rolling platforms. I dye my fabrics and do other messy work in our new garage, which is adjacent to the studio. Our Alaskan winters can be long and dark, but winter is also prime studio time for me. I love that I have a wall of south-facing windows, which invite the sun in during the day, and banks of full-spectrum lights that keep my space light and cheery when the sun fades. It is a bright and happy place to work.

Some Things Are Not Easily Seen: Poverty

by **Kathryn Upitis**

Sometimes there are quilts that just call out to us to make them. This was one of those quilts. United Way Canada had launched a campaign to have people stop and take a look at domestic violence, poverty, unemployment and homelessness—pervasive issues affecting Canadians. It was this campaign that gave me the inspiration to create this quilt for the American Patchwork and Quilting Two-Color Challenge for QuiltCon 2019, where it received Judge's Choice.

Poverty is right here, right in front of us all, each and every day, and yet we often don't recognize it or we choose not to see it. We know that one in ten Canadians live in poverty. It impacts each and every one of us, and each and every city across Canada. Many Canadians living in poverty face difficult decisions about things that most of us take for granted. This quilt asks viewers to challenge their perspectives. ✻

upitisquilts.com
@kupitis

"My mission was for this quilt to be seen—and now it will be travelling the world."

ERIN WILSON

I make quilts rooted in hand-dyed colour, architectural imagery and intricate piecework. As a self-taught textile artist, I've developed a method of small-scale patchwork that is both precise and improvisational. I've had solo exhibitions at the KOFU showroom in NYC, the Art Quilt Gallery NYC and International Quilt Week Yokohama in Japan, and have been a regular exhibitor at fine craft shows such as the American Craft Council Show in Baltimore, the Philadelphia Museum of Art Craft Show and the Smithsonian Craft Show. In addition to quiltmaking, I make custom soft goods for interior designers, and have worked in theatrical puppet design and fabrication with Chris Green Kinetics and as a sample maker for a technical military combat apparel manufacturer. Preceding and overlapping my career as a seamstress, I received a BFA in dance from the Juilliard School and performed as a modern dancer for 10 years. Originally from Indianapolis, Indiana, I live and work in a hand-built home in Brooklyn, New York.

"I use machine piecing, exclusively. I like the pureness of the single technique and enjoy working within the structure of piecing. It has become my language."

What is your personal relationship or history with quilts? What draws you to them? What led you to the world of quilts?

My mother taught me to sew when I was three or four. Her world was sewing and fibre art, and I took to it very quickly, but also I grew up in a house full of all types of materials and projects, not just sewing. She made quilts for our beds, and I made a few traditional quilts using calicos, but it wasn't until I was introduced to the world of contemporary artistic quilt making that I got really interested. Mom bought a few books on fabric dyeing (I was in high school by then), and the seed was planted. I knew little of the larger context and history of quilts, or art, for that matter. I was very much

FULL QUILT PHOTOS AND STUDIO PORTRAITS: BLACK AND STEIL

focused on the experience of making. The quilt form was ideal for my affinity to fabric and colour.

Now, quiltmaking is the core of my livelihood and creative expression, though I might say it has evolved into something closer to illustration and storytelling. The imagery in my work has become much more specific, narrative and personal.

What are your intentions when making a quilt or starting a creative project? What thought processes do you typically go through?

First I choose my colour palette, either from existing fabrics or by dyeing a new batch. There's no scientific method to this—it works best to go by instinct. Then, I cut strips of each fabric, pile them next to the sewing machine and begin. My quilts are almost always grids of small units. I make the blocks one by one, building a collection until I've either met the required dimensions or time's run out. The blocks are arranged and revised if needed, and the piece is assembled and finished.

What mindset or attitude do you think is best for quilting? How does quilting affect your mental and physical health?

Patience. Focus. Comfort with repetition. Not being too attached to original plans. When I am working well, I feel sharp and satisfied. More often, though, it's a fitful, frustrating, soul-searching process.

As for physical health, sitting at the machine all day isn't the greatest. I pay attention to my posture, get up frequently to move around and am always having to release my tense neck and jaw and shoulders.

Have you ever had a quilting or creative failure? What happened? What did you learn from it, if anything?

Failure is a constant presence. Technical mishaps. When I stitch a seam and miss the alignment: rip it out and try again, several times if need be—this is very normal. The night before a show the cat claws a hole in a piece or the iron spits brown water on a white quilt: disassemble, replace the damaged area, put it back together. Missed deadlines: communicate with the customer, and try to stop scheduling based on how long I think it should take instead of how long it actually takes. Rejection letters: oh well, try again next time.

Fear of failure is far more crippling, and this is usually about the internal creative side—what if I can't find the ideas? What if I can't produce enough? What if it's awful? These thought patterns are exhausting and counterproductive and very difficult to escape. I've been through long periods of burnout and the most recent round had me frozen. I stepped away from an intense show schedule and worked part-time at an outside job that was engaging but not creatively demanding. I learned new skills, and gave my art brain a rest—basically forced a change. I'm still in this place and slowly finding my way back into full-time quilt work. The lesson is always to keep moving through.

"It's not a conscious connection, but I believe there are elements of dance—musicality, timing, acute spatial awareness, the ritual aspect of training and practice—that carry through to my particularly intense version of quiltmaking. Both endeavours have been long roads, requiring lots of devotion."

In your opinion or experience, how does the act of quilting bridge the past, present and future?

I remember looking at a book of Illinois Amish quilts and seeing one in particular that felt related to my work at the time—like a crazy quilt but organized into squares—and thinking about how we keep making

WORKSPACE

I've almost always worked from home, and while it can be difficult to put aside life distractions, I prefer having everything under one roof and the ability to work late into the night. There's a large work table with a cutting mat to cover the entire surface. My design wall is covered in felt-wrapped homasote. There is a bulletin board with ideas and mementos and to-do lists, bookshelves, a cluttered desk with computer and papers. Windows on two sides, though I tend to close the curtains and turn on overhead work lights, as natural light (as much as I prefer it) makes it difficult to see colours clearly. For my sewing setup, the ironing board is at sitting height, so when I'm at the machine it's to my left. Each seam is sewn, trimmed and immediately pressed. There are scissors, a seam ripper, a pencil, a ruler, a notebook and piles of fabrics on the table. It gets very messy. Also, *three* cats.

the same discoveries about how to assemble fabric, many years and miles apart. While it felt new to me, it was not new to the world. Ideas are recycled and built upon, and I expect it will always be this way. I enjoy this kinship, knowing my stitches connect me to a very long lineage.

Would you consider yourself as a professional within the quilting industry? What breadth of activity and responsibilities do you have as a professional quilter?

When I was about 24 years old, I applied to a few juried craft fairs, got in, and that was my start. My work was received well enough that I knew I was onto something, and I found great fulfillment in making and selling, and in the direct in-person exchange with visitors and customers. A lot can be learned while standing in a booth with one's work for a weekend, and it is an intensely social experience compared to my usual solitary existence.

I sell my quilts, mostly to individuals and occasionally for public and commercial venues. I don't

teach or lecture or write books or patterns, etc. I mostly operate outside the "quilt world."

I sell my own work primarily through craft shows and commissions, do occasional contract work for other artists (including theatre and sculpture) and do custom sewing for interior designers. I've also worked as a sample maker for military gear—a fascinating job.

What motivates and inspires you?

Living a handmade life. Thriving as an independent artist and craftsperson. Building meaningful connections through art and creativity. Colours and shapes. Simply put, the making. I am a maker. ✻

"Imagery begins in a sketchbook with simple line drawings, but the process is mostly intuitive, with design and construction happening together. These quilts tell abstracted stories—informed by architecture, geometry, pattern and scenes from everyday life."

erinwilsonquilts.com
@erinwilsonquilts

HEIDI STAPLES

I've spent my life dabbling in various arts: drawing, cross-stitch, painting, ceramics. Nine years as an elementary teacher and one more as an assistant principal allowed me to bring my creativity into the schools where I worked, but it wasn't until I became a stay-at-home mom that I discovered the world of quilting. My husband and I decided to buy a home with my parents after our oldest was born so that none of us would have to rent any longer.

Four years later, my days were full as I did my best to keep up with three active little girls. I was happy but exhausted, struggling with the lack of creativity in my life. When I stumbled onto the online quilting community and then my mother brought a new sewing machine into our home, it seemed like it was all meant to be. I sewed my first quilt from an online tutorial and was so happy with the results. One quilt led to another. I began writing my blog, Fabric Mutt, to share my work with family, but it quickly became a way to connect with other quilters who shared my passion. It started me on a journey that I never could have imagined. I've sewn samples for a number of fabric companies, had my work published in various magazines, written two books and designed three fabric collections. It's all been a joy, and I'm so grateful for every opportunity I've been given!

"I love the harmony and simplicity of quilts, the idea of taking small broken pieces and sewing them back together to make something beautiful. I love that even when we sew by machine, we're still doing it with our hands and our hearts. The entire process is so personal from beginning to end."

How would you describe your style or aesthetic?

It took me a long time to figure out my style. I would attend Quilt Market, look at all the incredible artistic offerings there, and be embarrassed by my own work, which felt so simple and naive in comparison. I was talking about this with a friend once, sharing my

"I usually start with the purpose in mind. Once I know who I'm sewing for and why, it's much easier for me to choose the the project I want to make and find the right fabric for the pattern."

worries with her that maybe I didn't belong in this world of professionals when my work was so amateurish. "No, it's not," she insisted. "Your work is approachable." It was an important moment for me because my creative purpose finally snapped into focus. For the first time, I realized that simplicity is nothing to be ashamed of.

I enjoy simple patchwork because it allows the fabric to take centre stage and lets me take my work in any direction—traditional, modern, whimsical, etc. I design for people who love fabric. The pattern is our starting place, but the fabric is where we really make it our own. My style is "friendly." I want people at all sewing levels to say, "Hey, I could do that!" I want beginners to feel like they can try my tutorials without being intimidated, and I want advanced quilters to feel like they can take a break from more complicated projects to have fun with one of my patterns.

What mindset or attitude do you think is best for quilting? How does quilting affect your mental and physical health?

Even though much of my sewing is done to meet professional deadlines, I try to start early and work ahead as much as I can because it's really hard to be creative under pressure. I like to know that I can take my time and not have to settle for less than my best because I'm in a hurry. It's crazy how much time I put into some projects, spending hours to find the right fabrics and arrange them the way I think they look best, but when things fall into place, it's such a thrill. You just know when it's right, and it's the best feeling in the world. There's no doubt in my mind that quilting is good for the soul. I enjoy the process from beginning to end, and I love the feeling of contentment I get as I work.

I believe with all my heart that you must make what you love. Never, never sew with a pattern or fabric just because everyone else is doing it unless you truly love it yourself. Life is too short to squander your creative time on pleasing other people or trying to fit in with the crowd. And sewing should be fun. If it's not fun, it's not your hobby—it's just work.

Have you ever had a quilting or creative failure? What happened? What did you learn from it, if anything?

There are always going to be days when nothing seems to work the way I want it to. Persistence is a wonderful thing, but there's no virtue in needlessly banging my head against the wall. It's okay to walk away from a project for a while and come back later with a fresh perspective.

What quilt traditions do you hold dear? What quilting conventions do you ignore or challenge?

I will always love the tradition of making items for remembrance. We use and give handmade projects to celebrate important moments in our lives and in the lives of those we love. It's a part of our heritage as makers that will never go out of style. There's been so much conversation over the years about traditional versus modern quilting, and my view has always been that there's room enough in this family for all of us. If we're all making what we love and giving others the freedom to make what they love, we can celebrate our personal successes together without being sidetracked by

disagreements over how things should be done. Even if what you make isn't what I would make and vice versa, I can be glad that you find joy in your projects, and you can do the same for me. We can do things differently and still all agree that quilting makes us happy.

In your opinion or experience, how does the act of quilting bridge the past, present and future?

It gives me so much pleasure to quilt a project by hand, knowing that women were doing this hundreds of years ago and there will be others doing it for hundreds of years to come. It's an unbroken chain of creative joy. The styles and methods might change, but that desire to create beauty stays the same

When and how did you become a professional?

I didn't think of myself as a professional for a long time, partly because most of the sample sewing and blog posting I did was on my own time for no pay. Back then the excitement of working with new fabric and patterns was enough for me. It wasn't until I wrote my first book that I felt like I was stepping beyond the "hobbyist" label into something new. There are trade-offs to that, of course. When your hobby becomes your job, you're suddenly left without a hobby.

I've learned that I need to give myself time to both work and play in my sewing room. Know your priorities and stick to them no matter what; they're your guideposts, and you'll get lost without them. Remember that the world will not come crashing down if you don't do everything yourself, and it's okay to say no to some things—even good things—if the benefits aren't worth the sacrifices. And don't take yourself too seriously; keep things in perspective. When I was drowning in the pressures of writing my first book, my mother told me, "Heidi, it's an amazing thing that you got to write this book, and you'll always be able to look back

and be glad that you had the chance to do it. But don't ever forget that the book is just something you did. It isn't who you are." Sometimes I still need that reminder. I love my work, but there's more to me than that.

What breadth of activity and responsibilities do you have as a professional quilter?

I've done a little bit of everything. I've written over 40 free tutorials for my blog, Fabric Mutt, and many patterns for magazines, including *Love Patchwork and Quilting*, *Quilts and More* and *American Patchwork and Quilting*. I've written two books: *Sew Organized for the Busy Girl*, for C&T Publishing, and *Patchwork USA*, for Lucky Spool Media. I've designed three fabric collections for Riley Blake Designs: Five and Dime, Date Night and Shortcake. I've taught classes in California, Texas and Missouri.

Sometimes it seems like I'm facing a learning curve that's beyond my abilities, but I keep pressing forward. The more you do, the more you learn what you want to do and what you're good at, and that helps,

"Colour and fabric are always inspiring to me. I love learning how to do new things or how to do things in a different way. I'm a thematic person, which is why I have so much fun writing books and designing fabric. It's the story or theme behind the work that fascinates me, and I love bringing people into that world and helping them see what I see."

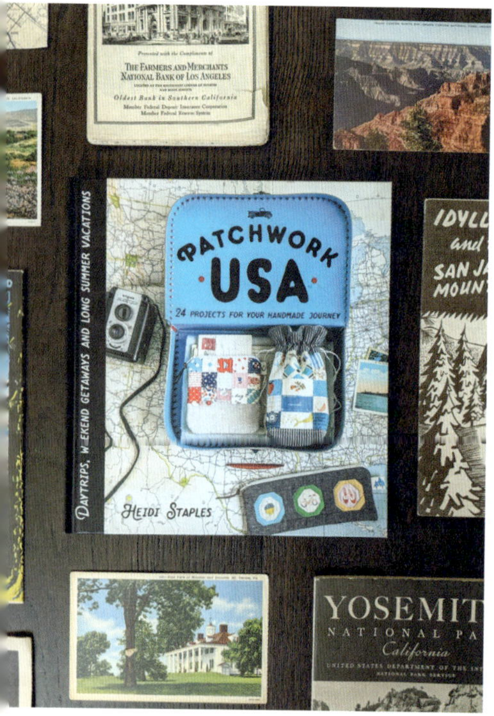

too. In this business—as in every business, I guess—you need a thick skin when it comes to taking criticism and rejection. Learn from mistakes, be willing to listen to advice from people who know what they're talking about, and don't be afraid to pursue opportunities. Four out of five times you may be ignored or rejected when you ask for the chance to do something, but there's always that one "yes," and it feels amazing! I'm the kind of person who wants to try everything at least once, and then if I feel like I'm not strong in an area, I can let that go and move on to something else that's a better fit. It takes time to find your spot, but it's worth it.

Are you able to support yourself in the quilt industry or do you have other endeavours as well?

I can't support myself on these jobs alone, unfortunately, but they've definitely been a blessing to our family budget. I'm still grateful that I can earn something while doing this creative work, and every little bit helps.

Do any particular ideas, objects or activities—outside of and unrelated to quilting—inform and inspire your quilting practice?

I'm enormously influenced by vintage style from the 1930s to 1950s. I love the fashion, packaging, advertising, movies and music from that era, and we have lots of it in our home. I read voraciously on many different topics, including design. It keeps me curious and well rounded, and I like to be both. My three daughters have always been a big part of my work. Many of my early projects were made for them, and as they've gotten older, they still love to watch me create projects, give me design advice and sew with me whenever we can manage it. ✻

fabricmutt.blogspot.com
@fabricmutt

WORKSPACE

I actually have three workstations in our home! The first is my teacher's desk, where I grade papers and tutor my daughters, since we home school them. It's a great setup because it allows me to spend so much time with my girls but also gives me the freedom to do my creative work on the side. In our guest room I work on my computer to create fabric collections and sewing patterns. I keep a set of files in there to organize my patterns, sketches and design inspiration. My sewing workspace in our upstairs loft is by far the largest area. That's where I keep my sewing machine, cutting and ironing stations, and a large fabric stash organized by substrate and colour. I have vintage art and objects at each of these spaces—many of which have been passed on or gifted to me by family—and I love seeing all that colour and glorious design everywhere I look. Getting to do my work in my own home is the best of all worlds for me. I get to have fun and be creative while spending my days with the people I love most. It just doesn't get any better than that.

PERFORMANCE ART

We Are Responsible for Our Dreams

by **Kevin Clancy**

This 21-by-21-foot tessellated blanket fort, my first quilt, was made for a month-long slumber party tour called We Are Responsible for Our Dreams. The project was a nomadic platform for collective dreaming, shared experience and utopian visioning.

Over 50 dream sessions were organized over the course of the project, including overnight slumber parties, group discussions, live sound collages, classes, film screenings, picnics, "seeing" sessions, open social spaces and sunrise group kirtan chants. Dream sessions occurred in private homes, art spaces, islands, universities, public parks, DIY basements, theatres and beaches in Pittsburgh, Boston, Cambridge, Worcester, Providence, New York City, Martha's Vineyard, Grand Rapids, Ann Arbor and rural Maine.

We Are Responsible for Our Dreams packs into a suitcase and will continue to circulate around the world on a perpetual tour. ✻

kevinclancy.studio
@kevinclancy.studio

JEN BROEMEL

I am Jen Broemel. I was a creative kid, an architect, a stay-at-home mom, a quilter and now basically a creative kid again. I am an artist and I am so grateful to have found quilting and my artistic passion—exploring in my own way, improvisationally with quilted cloth. My desire is to inspire others to experiment, explore and discover their creative thing and follow their passion.

I have always been drawn to the history and tradition of women sewing and the community that has surrounded and supported them. I am fortunate to have found a wonderful tribe of women to sew with regularly. They have been so generous and supportive in providing creative encouragement and inspiration.

I have really fallen in love with the process of quilting: the way in which the materials layer, the way they feel as they are worked, the way the thread and cloth come together, transforming and guiding the piece, adding texture, contrast and comfort with every stitch.

I began working with cloth for the vibrant colours and textures available in abundance. I was drawn to the idea of making with materials I had and could acquire easily, by repurposing fabric, old clothes and household linens. I love the idea of taking something ordinary, worn, used, and turning it into something special, something to cherish, to behold. Quilts to me have always been about putting together scraps of cloth. I have always been drawn to the creative ways in which quilters have historically made do, and decorated and comforted their families with cloth that they had on hand.

"I like to play, and I am not afraid to mess up. I set out with very little expectation of how a piece will turn out when I begin. I start with an idea, not a plan, and I enjoy every step of the way."

What are your intentions when making a quilt or starting a creative project?

My intention is to inspire others to look at the world around them more carefully, more mindfully, to see the extraordinary in the discarded, to notice the beauty in the mundane. How we see the world shapes our lives, our relationships, our actions. Let us notice the miracles of every day, every stitch. Every. Single. One.

What mindset or attitude do you think is best for quilting? How does quilting affect your mental and physical health?

I think it is important to have the mindset that there is no right way to do it. I think quilters can be so hard on themselves when things don't line up or turn out the way they planned. So many of my mistakes have led me to new explorations. I am grateful for them. I welcome them. They have helped me in all areas of my life. I am more patient and accepting of "what is." It has taught me to be more mindful; it is a meditative process for me and that has been very beneficial to me mentally and physically. The greatest gift it has given me, though, is the artistic passion that has me hopping out of bed every morning, eager to get to work. Having the desire to create has sparked a joy in me that has changed my life.

Have you ever had a quilting or creative failure? What happened? What did you learn from it, if anything?

I have creative failures every day. I see failure as an opportunity to get even more creative. I welcome failure. It means I am pushing myself to explore. You can not experiment and never fail. You can not grow and never fail. I do not fear failure, and because of that I have learned to find the bright side. It has been a blessing and a gift.

What quilt traditions do you hold dear? What quilting conventions do you ignore or challenge?

Taking pride in craftsmanship would be the quilt tradition that I cling to most. I will forever be honing my skills at the craft. I have curated my process to include the parts of the making that I enjoy most and have eliminated the parts I dread. I have figured out my way of doing things to make them more enjoyable to me, and often I am breaking the rules of tradition in doing so. Once I realized and owned that I was an artist making art and not a quilter making quilts, it was like a weight was lifted and I was free to explore new ways and new ideas of how to get the results I wanted. When I sit and sew with my tribe of experienced quilters and sewers, and they are inspired by my creations and impressed with my craftsmanship, it gives me the confidence to continue finding my own way.

"I especially love crazy quilts, and the makers who made them—they inspired me to work intuitively. I am grateful to have discovered these quilts, to have known from the beginning that there are many ways to make a quilt and express yourself through them."

In your opinion or experience, how does the act of quilting bridge the past, present and future?

I didn't consciously set out to find quilting; it found me. I am honoured to be able to contribute my work and to perhaps draw attention to the history of all the women who have used cloth and thread to make art—art that warmed and comforted their families, their communities, and decorated their lives. I am grateful to have learned from them how to explore, find and use my creative voice. I am

grateful for the freedom to use my voice the way I want, and I acknowledge that this is a relatively new freedom for women and that not all women have this freedom. It is a freedom that we must continue to protect and fight for.

The history of quilt making is long and complex. I am just getting started. I am still learning. My work is a little speck on the very textured timeline. But, still I am following my heart and creating art that is quilted. I am using my hands-on cloth and pursuing my art. Perhaps it will draw someone's attention to quilts and their history. Perhaps it will encourage someone to pursue their love of making quilts. Hopefully, it will embolden someone to use their voice and speak their mind. What else can we ask our work to do? This is how the world is changed every day. One little stitch at a time.

When and how did you become a professional?

I became a professional when I decided to dedicate my time and energy full time to my craft. I work at it; it is my job. It could pay a little better, but I sense a promotion coming (insert "laughing emoji" here).

I have begun dabbling in teaching workshops, sharing some of my techniques. Mostly, though, I want to inspire others to find and follow their own creative urges and desires. The work I make is for sale, so making the work, promoting the work and showing the work are the creative tasks of my day-to-day.

Are you able to support yourself in the quilt industry or do you have other endeavours as well?

I was an architect and became a stay-at-home mom after my third child was born. They are all in school now and I've realized that art really is what I want to pursue—and I am pursuing it like it is my full-time job. I have found ways to squeeze little part-time jobs in, too. I am grateful that it is not the other way around.

What motivates and inspires you?

I am motivated and greatly inspired by books. I'm a bit obsessed with reading about creativity, art and artists. The knowledge I've gained from books has helped me realize that I am an artist and has helped me become a confident one. I started an online book club (@fortheloveofyourart) to share some of the books that have meant a lot to me. I love passing it on and paying it forward. I know it will continue to inspire me and others.

When I began reading a lot on the subject of creativity and art making, meditation kept being recommended—so much so that I began to try it, and it has become a part of my creative practice, and extremely helpful to calming the craziness of my hectic life with three school-aged kids. ❇

WORKSPACE

My studio space is a mess. I am a messy maker and I don't love cleaning up. I don't mind the mess and I almost always know where most things are. I have space where I sew at the machine, and then I do a lot of my handwork at my dining room table so I can be more present with my family. I love that I have a dedicated space; it makes it so much easier to work at it regularly. I can stop when I need to stop and come back to it without setting up and putting things away. Hence the mess!

"I believe it is important to see real art in real life regularly and often. Its inspiration is inexplicable. There is no better way to get motivated and inspired to create than to look at, talk about and read about art."

jenbroemel.com
@highfivesandsilverlines

JODI GODFREY

I live in Castlemaine, Victoria, Australia (about an hour and a half north of Melbourne), with my husband and three kids. My friend Lucy and I laser cut English paper pieces in the boiler room of the old hospital that's now rented out as office and studio space.

Around the time my first child was born, I was living next door to a friend who made quilts. She was fun and haphazard and her quilts were, too. She would put together fabrics I wouldn't dream of using next to each other, fabric from her childhood, from thrift stores and from quilt shops, and all of her quilts were so beautiful. I'd long held this idea that creativity was reserved for the professional, or for people who'd been lucky enough to start when they were young and had been trained.

This constantly made me feel like something was missing from my life, because I longed for a kind of self-expression I couldn't put into words. My friend's quilts were so welcoming and unapologetic. They made me really want to try it myself. The first quilts I made were so basic and different from what I love to make now, but because I didn't have any preconceived notion of what a quilt should look like, and how I might be failing at it, I just kept making them.

"My business and family life is made up of a thousand tiny jobs a day, so the time I get to sew for long stretches, with a peaceful mind, is a real joy."

PHOTOGRAPHS BY JANE MCLEAN FROM *THE SEEDLING QUILTS*

What are your intentions when making a quilt or starting a creative project?

I have several different steps that are pretty separate from each other. I have pattern design time, which is all about shape and line. I do a little of this on the computer, but mostly it's with actual shapes in my hand. I'll take a bunch of shapes that relate to each other (in size and angles) and play with them at the table, discovering the different ways they can form patterns. I take photos as I go. Sometimes something sticks out to me immediately and I dive in quickly, but often they are just stored for later inspiration. I name my favourites and keep them in Trello (a list-making app). Often a design will sit for a long time in black-and-white before I have an inspiration for how to colour it in.

Then, from a different end, I might have a particular idea I'm trying to evoke, or I'm looking for a good match for a particular collection, or I'm thinking about a particular event—a launch or sew-along or club, and I'll go through old photos or the Trello list and see if there's a good match.

Or some days, the way to colour a quilt will come to me suddenly. I'll realize I've been holding off because I didn't want to use solids, or it was too close to another quilt I had in mind, but I could just drop that other one. When I get that moment of serendipity, I usually dive in and start cutting.

What mindset or attitude do you think is best for quilting? How does quilting affect your mental and physical health?

I think I do my best work when I'm tuned in to what I love, rather than what other people are loving at the moment. I also enjoy the whole process the most if I'm not on a deadline or contract. I like the freedom to be able to put something down if it's not working and come back to it six months later. I also do my best work if I'm not worried that I'm letting someone down.

For me, the health thing can go either way. I can push myself too hard and hurt my hands and back and head. My back always plays up when I've been stitching for a deadline. But sometimes pushing myself is a good challenge and really engaging, too. There's nothing quite like knowing "this is exactly what I should be doing right now," and being able to run with it.

Have you ever had a quilting or creative failure? What happened? What did you learn from it, if anything?

Ha! So many! I think quilting stuck with me because I didn't turn up with the expectation that I would be a genius at it early on. I'd been pretty impatient with myself from an early age that piano and drawing and songwriting didn't come easily to me. But I had no preconceived ideas about what a "good quilter" was because I'd had so little exposure to it. So I'd make a quilt and discover that I didn't like it, or it didn't look like I'd hoped, and instead of berating myself that I should have known, I just took note of what I could change and moved on to the next one.

That approach is great for learning what you like about colour and design, but the "not checking before cutting" mistakes are the hardest to live with! In my book, *The Seedling Quilts,* I made a quilt called Honeysuckle in which long vines are appliquéd to the whole cloth back and then trimmed after quilting. During the trimming, I didn't check properly and cut too much off the quilt. It made it landscape rather than portrait, and even though it was only an inch or so off, it completely changed the look of the quilt for me. Ugh! I put it away for three days before deciding to keep it and bind it. It's just a quilt. It didn't need to be perfect. It still did its job as it was.

"When it comes to colour, I love an 'all in' look. I love traditional geometry and repetitive patterns. Vintage quilt blocks and hexagons are just so beautiful!"

What quilt traditions do you hold dear? What quilting conventions do you ignore or challenge?

My most treasured quilting tradition is to use quilts as a means to tell one's story. For many women in the past, quilts were a real way to express their political opinion, support their local needy or share their history. Equally valuable was the way women used them as generous gifts to friends and to provide for their families. I have many more ways to speak up today, but I love to tell stories with my quilts.

I really love traditional patterns. I love that many were inspired by tiling and other designs from even further back. I feel so connected to a long line of creatives when I play with my shapes, come up with something new and then discover it in ancient Roman tiling or my quilt block encyclopedia!

I follow traditional methods of construction and order. Quilt blocks, quilt top, quilt sandwich, then quilt and bind. So when I stray from convention, it's usually to find ways that suit my rhythm or preferences. Some have just become the new convention, like using spray baste or glue sticks during construction. Some go back in the direction of older ways, like avoiding white, shiny cardboard templates and using only recycled paper, though admittedly laser cut rather than with scissors!

In your opinion or experience, how does the act of quilting bridge the past, present and future?

It's easy to feel alone in this life, to assume we're the only one who has certain struggles or desires, that other people are much happier or together. When I read about women and their quilts in the past, women who sewed their way through the Depression, or through pregnancy, or loss, or who sewed for their new home, who contributed block patterns to their local newspaper, or entered in the thousands to a nation-wide quilting competition run by a department store, I think: they were just like me!

I think the wealth of information, designs, pictures and stories that we've contributed online in the last decade or more will be the same kind of gift to future quilters.

Would you consider yourself as a professional within the quilting industry?

My husband, Tim, and I started our business three years ago when he built a laser cutter. We developed

an online store and started advertising our English paper piecing papers through my blog and Instagram feed, which I had started several years earlier as a hobby.

I tend to keep my roles to pattern design, quilt making and order fulfilment, but I've also taught classes, written a book, made a DVD with a local quilting magazine, contributed to other publications and done some freelance design for fabric manufacturers.

Are you able to support yourself in the quilt industry or do you have other endeavours as well?

I've just started to pay myself. Hurray! I made the decision to employ my friend Lucy, who makes quilts and cut orders with me, and my virtual assistant, Michelle, because family life is pretty unpredictable. I wanted to know things will continue making progress even if I'm home with sick kids. Some people would have done it the other way around, but I just knew I wouldn't get to sew if I did everything else. My husband works full time and that keeps the family budget ticking over.

Do any particular ideas, objects or activities—outside of and unrelated to quilting—inform and inspire your quilting practice?

I love learning about all kinds of history and art. I spend a lot of time looking at ancient tiling designs and other patterns. I find the stories related to the designs, and the way they interacted with the culture at the time, particularly interesting.

In my book, *The Seedling Quilts*, I researched medicinal herbs and the way they've been used throughout history, and then made quilts to evoke those stories and healing properties. ❇

"Having a vision for something inspires me. It might be as simple as knowing how I was to quilt it that motivates me to finish the top and baste it. Or it might be big and exciting, like a new idea for a club or collaboration. Quilts that don't have a 'reason' or aren't connected to the bigger picture tend to take much longer or end up in the destash pile."

WORKSPACE

I have a sewing room at home that is basically used as a storeroom because it's cold and dark. I do most of my stitching in the lounge room. Our workshop for cutting orders is a five-minute drive away. Working outside the home hasn't really worked for us. If something breaks down or a new code needs testing, Tim has to drive over after dinner and attend to it, and call me to ask questions because the kids are in bed. It's hard to work together because someone is always home with the kids. We're currently in the process of building a house with a studio attached. That will save us rent, and allow us to work with the family around. I can't wait!

talesofcloth.com
@talesofcloth

example
Love
FUNNY
zealous
Witty
STAUNCH
curious
OPINIONATED
bold
Honest
TOUGH
Steadfast
spirited
Efficient
Optimistic
STRONG
Resourceful
LOYAL
UNDEFEATED
SAGE
CURIOUS
assertive
Vocal
Courage
STRONG
APPREHENSIVE
Worthy
purposeful
Brave
Kindness
vote
sociable
enough
Vivacious
Educated
enough
resilient
possible
Capable
POWERFUL
curious
maker
good hearted
FORGIVING
Joy
RESILIENT
Peacemaker
CHAMPION
Inspired
HOPEFUL
BLESSED
warrior
Optimist
Steadfast
Steady
DRIVEN
Independent
Dedicated
Fearless
RESILIENT
devoted
inspired
artistic
BRAVE
RESOURCEFUL
Leader
Strong
Patience
valuable
DETERMINED
intrepid
important
Blessed
PASSIONATE
grateful
Feliz
Powerful
APASIONADA
caring
LOYAL
Conscientious
capable
Eloquent
Joy
quirky
hopeful
STEADFAST
crafty
TRY
headstrong
Unlimited
engrossed
curious
daring
RESILIENT
INTUITIVE
CONCERNED
RESPONSIBLE
ardent
OPTIMISTIC
HUMAN
Self Confident
generous
Kind
JOYÜ
minimalist
vibrant
AMPLIFIER
Enough
Independent
resolute
GENUINE
Mama
Creative
RADIENT
transforming
LovEd
Kind
patient
TENACIOUS
LOYAL
Unique
creative
Patience
DRIVEN
mindful
Gracious
Wise
hopeful
Creative
persistent
visible
HAPPY
resolute
strong
HOPEFUL
RESPECT
Generous
Loyal
Confident
patient
Soar
BOSS
Worthy
resilient
COURAGE
Maker
Dauntless
concrete
REBEL

In Our Own Words

by **Kim Smith Soper**

This collaborative quilt is a celebration of women, of the individual qualities that make us who we are, and of our strength when we come together in community. On International Women's Day 2018, I put out a call, asking women near and far to send me a hand-stitched word of empowerment that best describes them. The idea was to create a quilt that would acknowledge and honour ourselves in a positive way as we still work towards equality.

A total of 196 words were collected from across the world, each with the unique voice and personality of the woman who stitched it. As an unexpected bonus, I also received many beautiful letters explaining why the women chose the words that they did. They shared powerful stories of strength, pride, joy and grace. It was an honour to hold onto these words, and knowing the stories behind them made it even more meaningful.

Each word was placed in its own circle, which was a nod to femininity and the cycles of nature. The fabrics are wovens, to represent our soft but unwavering strength. The courthouse steps design with a fire burning at the hearth centre is an homage to quilters past and present. It was quilted by Shelly Paglia.

I am forever grateful to everyone who took the time to stitch a word and to share their story for this project. It is both a communal project and one that is deeply personal to me. Ultimately, I hope that this quilt can be seen as a tangible representation of our beauty, strength, creativity, individuality and commonality, told in In Our Own Words. ✻

lelandavestudios.com
@lelandavestudios

KRISTYNE CZEPURYK

I am the middle child of a regular middle-class family. My childhood was pretty normal. I did the usual things like Brownies and Girl Guides, piano lessons, skating, swimming, baseball, field hockey, and also lots and lots of crafting. I was terrible at pretty much every sport, which is probably why I ended up finding things to do that didn't require physical prowess.

I earned an English degree, and then a public relations diploma (because an English degree plus nothing else equalled not much I was interested in doing to earn a living). I got a few PR jobs, but learned quickly that I was not cut out to be interviewed for the six o'clock news.

I married a boy I met in high school. We weren't technically high school sweethearts because we started dating when I was in university (yes, I'm older than him). I settled into a quiet career as a technical writer until I became a mom of two beautiful girls.

Since re-entering the workforce six years ago as a technical writer, I also took night classes to become a certified graphic designer. So today I'm a wife and a mom with a full-time job. All my creative endeavours happen in my "spare time."

What is your personal relationship or history with quilts? What draws you to them? What led you to the world of quilts?

There are no quilters in my family tree, and there was only one quilt in my home growing up—my dad's baby quilt made of feed sacks by my grandmother's friend, in 1942. But I never paid much attention to that

"Whether your quilt is kept, used, loved by family or strangers into the future... that is not for the quilter to know. And I don't think it's the quilter's responsibility. They only need to make. Today."

raggedy old thing. (My mom had a love affair with bleach, and this poor quilt, although it was falling apart, was very white!) I own that quilt now and I treasure it dearly.

In junior high home ec class, I made a log cabin pillow. My poor mom was horrified that I'd spent $20 (in 1982) for barely enough fabric to make a pillow! But I got 100% on that project, so I instantly believed that quilting was something I might be good at.

In high school, I worked in the fabric department of a store (now Walmart) and spent a lot of time around pretty fabrics and notions. I think it was there that I first felt inspired to make a quilt.

Then when I was 18, I got a summer job working at a historical village, where I'd dress up like a girl from the 1910s and tell visitors (mostly tourists) about how people lived in the olden days. Part of my job was to engage in activities that were "authentic" to the time. I met a girl there (we are still good friends) who taught me how to English paper piece. I made my first hexagon quilt on the job that year, and I haven't stopped quilting since.

How would you describe your style or aesthetic?

With a single word: pretty!

What are your intentions when making a quilt or starting a creative project? What thought processes do you typically go through?

Intentions vary from project to project. Sometimes, I want or need to make a gift for someone special. Sometimes I am asked to promote fabric, or a pattern, or a book. Sometimes it's an obligation (like school fundraisers).

But my favourite intentions come from authentic creative inspiration—by fabric, by a pattern, by a shape, by a song, a colour, something I saw somewhere... Often it's just an instant impulse that seems to come from nowhere. Yes, the intentions to scratch a creative itch to simply make something pretty are the best intentions of all.

Once I'm struck with a desire to make something specific, I quickly run through a mental checklist of questions: Will it be pretty? Does it look like fun? Will I need to learn a new skill? Do I have all the supplies and tools I need? How challenging will it be? Will it be useful? Who can I give it to if I don't use it? The answers to these questions usually determine if I answer the call now, later or never.

What mindset or attitude do you think is best for quilting? How does quilting affect your mental and physical health?

Quilting is not so much a creative exercise as it is an essential part of my mental well-being. In my mid-teens, I thought it would be a good idea to challenge myself and finish my growing collection of works in progress. It seemed like the mature thing to do. So I cleared the decks and wiped my creative slate clean. I thought I would feel accomplished, satisfied, organized and proud when my to-do list was done.

But wow, was I ever wrong! Instead of all these positive things, I only found emptiness. I literally found nothing. No skill to improve. No problem to

solve. No activity to occupy my mind and fingers. No anticipation of a new challenge. No fantasizing about a beautiful thing I could make. It was awful. I tend to be a giggly, happy sort of person, and even my friends at school started asking what was wrong.

I didn't connect the dots right away between having nothing to make and feeling sad. But the second I did, I set about filling a new list of projects, and I've never had nothing to do, creatively, since then. That doesn't mean I'm always making. But having the option to make, having something waiting for me, having something to think about making when meeting life's other obligations... that's what I need to be happy.

That experiment so many years ago was the closest I've been to being depressed. It is with utter conviction that I say quilting is my antidepressant.

Have you ever had a quilting or creative failure? What happened? What did you learn from it, if anything?

I've had countless failures and disappointments throughout my quilting life. And I'm certain that as long as I'm quilting, I will continue to make mistakes. Sometimes these mishaps are an accidental surprise, and happily become part of the finished project. On the other hand, sometimes mistakes are ripped out, unpicked, cut off or otherwise unceremoniously removed.

And then there are the misfortunes that are kept. Only time will tell if they will, at best, be ignored or forgotten, or at worst, be regrettable and serve as a constant reminder of my failure to create with my hands the vision I held in my imagination.

Would you consider yourself as a professional within the quilting industry? When and how did you become a professional?

I kind of tiptoed my way into becoming a "professional" quilter. My first real pay cheque as a maker came when I was a stay-at-home mom with two little ones.

In 2004, I sold some gift items (patchwork bags, Christmas stockings and lavender sachets) on consignment in a pretty little gift shop. A year later, I got a job teaching quilting classes at a local quilt shop. There I quickly became a busy store sample maker, pattern writer, embroidery club leader and, eventually, project designer to help sell new fabric collections.

While I worked at the shop, I discovered Japanese quilting books and magazines, and was an instant junkie. I adore the craftsmanship, the designs, the smaller piecing, the handwork, the beautiful combination of quilting and embroidery... I loved it all. That solidified my penchant for small patchwork and bag making. (I was known as "the bag lady" at the shop.) These days I'm far more likely to design and make quilted pouches and totes as I am to sew a quilt.

I started a blog and an online shop selling my patterns in 2011. As my audience grew, more opportunities came my way, like monetizing my blog, writing magazine contributions, designing patterns for fabric manufacturers to promote new collections, and eventually writing my first book, *S is for Stitch*, in 2012.

WORKSPACE

When I turned 16, my mom and dad gave me a sewing machine and it lived on a bookshelf in my bedroom. I had to clear the desk in my room when I wanted to sew, and my fabric and pattern storage were limited to space under my bed. I've also known the inconvenience of having the kitchen table as the only place to sew. But about five years ago, my husband and I built our current home. The top floor is a 450-square-foot loft with windows on every wall, hardwood floors, and white walls and ceiling. My husband has one corner for his desk, and I get the rest of the space for all of my designing, sewing and making. I'm so grateful for this space because I can have multiple projects on the go, I don't have to move things out of anyone's way and I can easily move from fabric pulling to cutting, to pressing, to sewing, to pattern writing, to photography, all in one happy place.

I guess that's when I considered myself officially "professional." Since then I've been fortunate enough to fulfill what I once thought was an impossible dream to design fabric... Having your name on a selvage!

Are you able to support yourself in the quilt industry or do you have other endeavours as well?

I've always kept my quilting work as a side hustle. I quickly learned that I'm skilled on the creative side, but not driven as an entrepreneur. Turning my creative passion into a necessary income seems to rob the joy for me. So I have my full-time job as a technical writer to pay the bills, and my side hustle to feed my soul.

What motivates and inspires you?

I think all creatives have something in common, and that's an indescribable, innate need to make. We aren't satisfied or fulfilled if we aren't—at any given moment, either consciously or unconsciously—involved in something creative.

For me, it's like lightning strikes a little part in my brain and triggers an irresistible desire to make something. I'll see something that will spark my imagination and I'll envision something really pretty in my head that I need to turn into something real. I need this thing to exist. And I need to be the one to bring it to life. ✻

prettybyhand.com
@prettybyhand

LATIFAH SAAFIR

In many ways, I am still that 17-year-old mechanical engineering student that used to sneak off to take merchandising and design classes to maintain my sanity. In a world that often tries to push us in one direction or another in our careers, little did I know that becoming a quilter and running a business as a quilt educator and product developer would be the perfect solution, making all the parts of my brain and heart happy.

What is your personal relationship or history with quilts? What draws you to them? What led you to the world of quilts?

I was the weird teenager who was enamoured with quilts and would check out every quilting book from the Weatherford Public Library. For some reason, the closest I came to quilting then was making a denim patchwork quilt top out of sx-inch denim squares recycled from discarded clothing from my five siblings. Sandwiched on top of a comforter, it became the quilt I slept under in college. No one around me quilted, though I understand at least one of my great-grandmothers did. I was just always drawn to it.

It wasn't until I was in my early thirties that I made my first real quilt. I saw a quilt—also made of recycled materials—made by a new friend, Jen Tierney, and finally knew I needed to be quilting. I used a tutorial on the Purl Soho blog, bought fabric from the then $1.79 flat fold section, bought a new Kenmore and made my first quilt. My tendency to be a serial crafter made me question my longevity in quilting. So my only goal was to finish it. This lead me to the online modern quilting world, which opened up so many new possibilities. That year I went to Quilt Festival in Long Beach and walked the floor alone. That experience of not seeing

"I am motivated to quilt because I need to get these ideas out of my head and out into the world."

much from the vibrant online modern quilt world in real life sparked a series of events that resulted in the formation of the Los Angeles Modern Quilt Guild and eventually the Modern Quilt Guild.

"I'm constantly inspired by accidental beauty and environments, no matter if they are traditionally beautiful or not. I've always found beauty in random spaces. I love graffiti and street art. I love exploring art and colour in various cultures."

How would you describe your style or aesthetic?

I'm pretty sure the world describes me as a modern quilter, but I like to just call myself a quilter. I have a love/hate relationship with labels and the subsequent boxes we put ourselves and others in. I'm okay with the "quilter" box—for now. It is a self-imposed box so that I won't scatter my creative energy too far around. Because in my heart of hearts I just love making and creating almost anything. I'm intrigued by wood and metal and paint and glass and... In my mind, I design furniture and garments and paint beautiful pictures. For now, I corral all of that in and I'm just a quilter. I just make what my heart calls me to make and I try to stay true to that.

What are your intentions when making a quilt or starting a creative project? What thought processes do you typically go through?

To finish it. Eventually. Sadly, I'm not a quilter who always enjoys the process. My joy in quilting is to see the vision in my head come to life.

What mindset or attitude do you think is best for quilting? How does quilting affect your mental and physical health?

I try to embrace quilting with a child's mind—a mind of play and exploration, and void of this attitude that we have to be perfect. I seek excellence and not perfection. I want a finished product I can be proud of, so I invest time in developing skills to make that happen easily. But I rein in my perfectionist side and choose when to let her out. Perfection has a place but can quickly kill the creative spirit.

Have you ever had a quilting or creative failure? What did you learn from it, if anything?

All the time. I recently posted a meme that says "Seam Ripping is my Superpower." I end one of my design lectures with a quote from graphic designer Paula Scher that says, "It's through mistakes that you actually can grow. You have to get bad in order to get good." I think our attitude around perceived failure defines who we are as makers. I always encourage my students to get bad. We celebrate it. Revel in it. Encourage it even. Dance around and play in it. This is what releases the magic. Or at least frees us to create.

What quilt traditions do you hold dear? What quilting conventions do you ignore or challenge?

Community is one of the strongest traditions in quilting. But as the founder of a guild and as someone who travels to dozens of guilds across the country, I find that our greatest strength can also be our greatest weakness.

Keep (and/or instill): Kindness. Inclusion. Safety. Learning. Support. Friendship. Quilting. Remove: Judgement. Cliques. Mean girls and boys.

In your opinion or experience, how does the act of quilting bridge the past, present and future?

I think of quilting as creating morsels of beauty to wrap around those we love. I make quilts for those in the world I consider my family—both born into and chosen. And in spite of years that pass by and technology and tools and advancement, at the end of the day we're still just cutting up fabric and sewing it back together. Just like the generations of the past. It is timeless and universal in that it creates a beautiful, functional object whose primary role is to create warmth and comfort.

When and how did you become a professional? What breadth of activity and responsibilities do you have as a professional quilter?

I got laid off of my "real job" working for a Fortune 500 company in 2013 and I used that as a gift to move into something that I loved more. I am still building but I've been working exclusively in this industry for the last couple years.

I look at myself as both a quilting educator and a product developer. I design patterns, templates, tools and fabric. I'm a travelling quilt teacher.

I work with other amazing entrepreneurs in our industry. Alison Schmidt does brilliant technical editing for my patterns. I worked with the amazing Annabel Wrigley from Little Pincushion Studio on my most recent Quilt Cadets patterns to teach kids to sew. Samarra Khaja blessed me with some of her amazing graphic design skills for Quilt Cadets as well. And the ladies from Page + Pixel did the covers. Working with other talented people, we all shine brighter! ✻

"As a small business owner, so far I do most of it: packing product, designing product and packaging, pattern layouts, order fulfillment, invoicing, and on and on. I'm looking forward to taking the next step and being able to hire some help."

WORKSPACE

We are helping my 99-year-old grandfather through his golden years and decided to live in his home with him to not take him out of his environment. So, I primarily sew on a portable sewing table in my bedroom. I also shoot my YouTube videos there in a "studio" that can be put up and taken down in a corner of the bedroom. It can be frustrating at times but it definitely shows that you can create and flourish in any situation.

latifahsaafirstudios.com
@latifahsaafirstudios

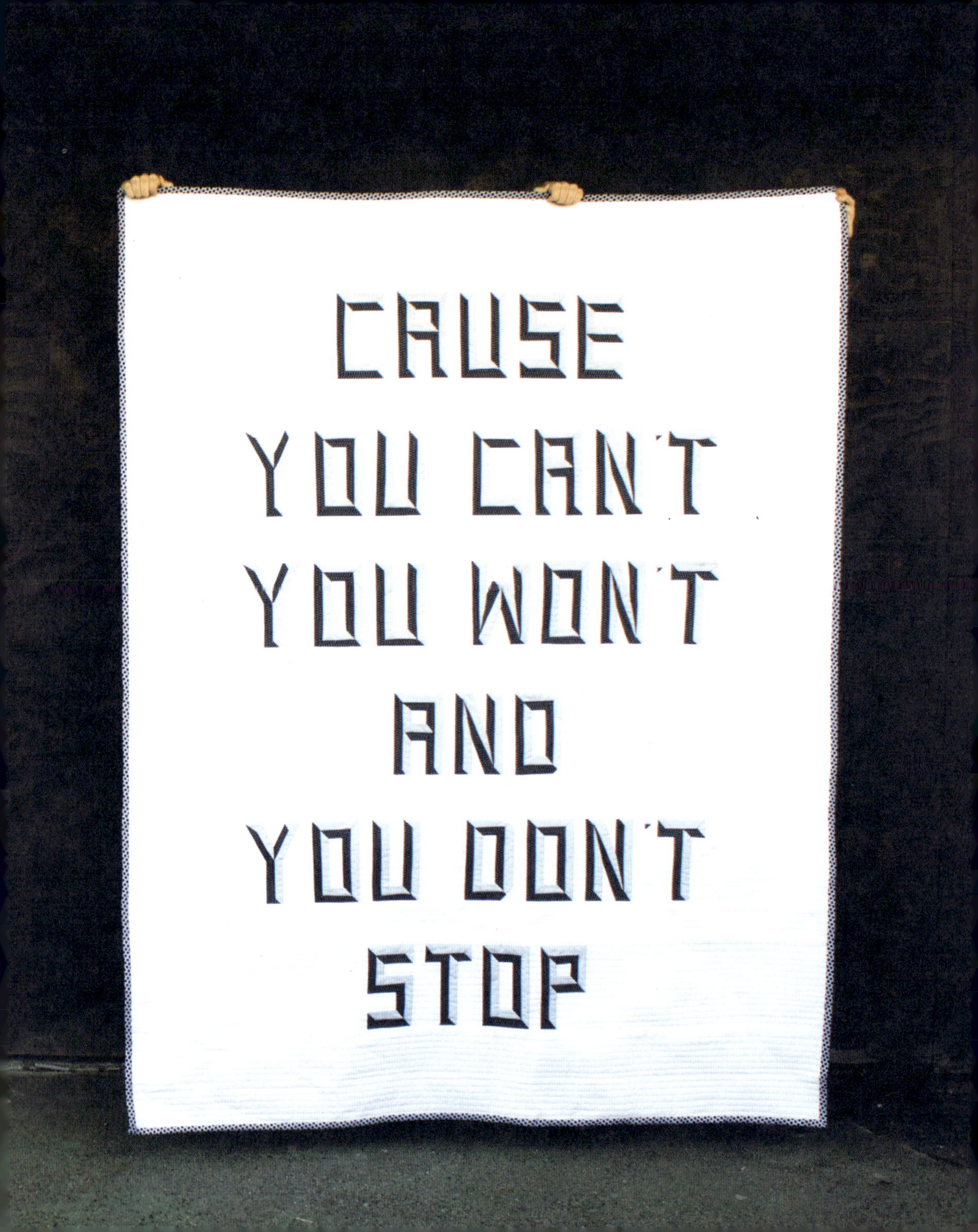
CAUSE
YOU CAN'T
YOU WON'T
AND
YOU DON'T
STOP

Cause you can't, you won't and you don't stop

by **Lysa Flower**

I hit a wall in late 2017. The joy I felt making all of a sudden felt challenging (and not in a fun way). It didn't make sense. Had I exhausted myself? The past few years had been an explosion of creative growth: learning Adobe Illustrator, learning surface pattern design, showing and designing my modern sewing patterns. This year had been the best one yet! An amazing year, in fact. I sewed for Kim Kight's Snap to Grid collection, creating a Boombox sewing machine cover, a Cassingle quilt and my cassette tape mini quilt. I went to St. Louis for Quilt Market, and met Kim and other amazing people. I released my Boombox and Cassingle patterns, plus released tutorials for my cassette tape book cover, a cassette tape zippy pouch and the Boombox sewing machine cover. How could I be stuck now? I was on a roll! Dang it! Where did the momentum go? How do I navigate this?

No matter how I was feeling, the Quiltcon submission deadline was fast approaching. What was I going to make for that? Would I be able to make anything?

I decided to play with a text-based pattern I was developing. I began to sift through my records in search of inspiration. I opened the Beastie Boys album *Ill Communication*. I had only read a few lines before I found it, like a punch in the stomach… in a good way. The lyrics struck me: "'Cause you can't, you won't and you don't stop." I knew I had found the text for the quilt and I had found my answer to this creative block I had been grappling with. The most important thing was not to stop; quitting was not an option. It has become my mantra and an extra big, quilt-sized note to self. ✻

lysaflower.com
@lysaflower

LAURA PETROVICH-CHENEY

My name is Laura Petrovich-Cheney. I was born in Philadelphia and grew up in a little town called Haddonfield, New Jersey. My childhood summers were spent at the beach, or as they say in Jersey, "the shore." For nearly 20 years, my husband and I lived in Asbury Park. After Hurricane Sandy in 2012, our community and lives changed so much. The little bungalows were rebuilt into McMansions, and recognizable faces were replaced with strangers. Besides, my parents both died shortly after the hurricane, and the year before, my husband's brother and sister-in-law died. These years were just riddled with loss, sorrow and death. We were desperate for a change, something hopeful and new. In 2017, we sold our Jersey home and moved to Marblehead, a quiet coastal town in New England, where we hope to never see another hurricane.

My interests are varied. I enjoy beekeeping, visiting national parks, watching professional hockey, hiking, cooking and gardening. An avid museum-goer, I study women artists almost exclusively because we are so underrecognized. I love reading books, fiction and nonfiction, that deal with Medieval Europe and the American Civil War. I consider myself a gym rat and secretly want to teach Zumba.

"I always strive to make my quilts individualistic pieces of art and to close the gap between craft and art, women's work and men's work."

WOODWORKING

Developing the skills I need to accomplish my best work didn't happen overnight and hasn't happened yet. Art school introduced me to woodworking, but the real work happens every day in the studio. Good woodworking is more than just "measure twice, cut once." I've learned that almost every mistake can be fixed, to never skimp on sanding and to use the right tool for the job. Safety is paramount. But most importantly, my wood quilts have taught me to give up on perfection.

I long for perfection more than anything in my work—that ideal masterpiece. But the wood absorbs moisture when humidity is present and/or shrinks when the air is dry. The wood is always alive. Pieces never quite lay perfectly together. Height variations can alter things, too.

If I truly aimed for perfection, I would still be working on my first or second piece. I have learned to accept the imperfections in the work. Wood is a good teacher—both in the studio and in life.

What is your personal relationship or history with quilts? What draws you to them?

Like many of us, my childhood looked pretty wonderful from the outside, but inside there was plenty of discontent and dysfunction. To ease my loneliness and help manage things, I turned to books. I had some pretty meaningful relationships with the people and animals in those novels. Sometimes I wanted to be the main character—like in the Little House on the Prairie book series. Laura and I not only shared a name, but we both had red hair and freckles, and were always up to something. Mostly, I wanted to be Laura because she felt loved by her family, and even though her life seemed challenging, the outcomes were positive and hopeful. One of the most visceral connections I had to the Little House stories was the fabric, sewing and quilts. The visuals of those quilts touched something in me. I can't say really why the quilts meant so much to me in the stories, but they did. I wished for my life to be filled with quilts like Laura's. At nine years old, I can remember walking past my town's quilt store feeling like Laura going to the general store. I just fell in love in the calico fabrics—the little roses and daisies, the soft colours, the fresh smell of the fabric, the thump sound of unravelling bolts on the cutting table, the swish-snap of the scissors. All these sensations—tactile and emotional—just got bundled up as "quilt." I began to associate quilts with comfort and love.

What is your creative process in beginning a wood quilt?

I am drawn to the complexity of patterns and enjoy figuring out how I can translate fabric and sewing into wood. The complexity determines how much prep time I need before I start. So many quilt designs are rectangular—which makes sense because beds are rectangular. However, I prefer my pieces to be square. The first step is to draw the piece out on graph paper. Erasing pencil marks on paper is much easier than reworking a wood sculpture.

Once the size of the piece is determined, I prepare the backing boards. People often ask me how I pick the size of the finished work, and my answer is simple: I am limited to whatever I can get at the lumber yard. The backing boards are primed and painted, usually grey or black. If the mood strikes me, I paint them a bright colour. Once I have worked out the mathematics of the pieces on graph paper, I draw the design on the backing board. The salvaged wood pieces are then glued to these finished backing boards. Occasionally, I work without a plan—like a provisional quilt.

What led you to create quilts made from wood?

After a nor'easter, my dog and I found two wrecked orange and turquoise wood boats that had washed up on the beach. Drawn in by the bright colours, I hauled the boats into my truck, and they sat in my studio for a year.

In the recess of my imagination, I had spent a great deal of time wondering how to combine fabric with woodworking. Then, in a grocery store line, I flipped through a decorating magazine and had my ah-ha moment. There was an orange and turquoise quilt that reminded me of my boats. Once home, I started to hack up those boats with a saw. After days of cutting and sanding, I figured out how to make a wooden quilt.

For the next months, I was using up that wood. Then Hurricane Sandy hit and my wooden quilt series developed into something more meaningful. Scattered in the streets were wooden remnants of the neighbourhoods and people's lives. I picked up the pieces of rubble—broken dressers, shattered kitchen cabinets, twisted screen doors, cedar siding. American patchwork quilts were designs that I found familiar and comforting. This reassurance was especially significant. My father died shortly after the storm; my mother, six months later.

Since Sandy, I have witnessed countless more storms. These storms are great equalizers. We all suffer loss, regardless of our colour, language or economic status. Our hearts break equally and painfully. I believe that sharing this story through quilts connects us and makes us vulnerable, fully human and whole.

Have you ever had a quilting or creative failure? What happened? What did you learn from it, if anything?

My biggest failure was my first quilt. I dragged my mother to a local quilt show. There was a beautiful yellow calico quilt for sale—the kind of quilt I imagined Laura Ingalls would have had. I longed for that sunny, bright, happy quilt as only a 15 year old could. All the begging and negotiating in the world couldn't convince my mother to buy it. Heartbroken, I decided there could be another way to get a quilt. I saved my babysitting money and bought a used sewing machine, a *Quilt in a Day* book and fabric—mostly yellow. Everything was expensive and there was no way that I was wasting fabric on "seam allowances." So, I sewed my pieces as close to the edge as possible. My quilt was a success and it was even a little bigger than expected. Up until the moment I washed the quilt and the seams gave way, I thought I was genius.

In regard to my wood quilts, I made several mistakes over the years—the wrong glue, the wrong backing, not sanding enough, cutting before measuring. But these mistakes were never as horrific as my seams coming apart. So often what I do now is experimental and there are no directions to follow. I must rely on coming to terms with failure and disappointment. What keeps me going and striving for good work is that 15-year-old girl's persistence and determination; they are still hallmarks of my work ethic.

What quilt traditions do you hold dear? What quilting conventions do you ignore or challenge?

When I first started quilting, I was interested in their functionality. While making something warm and cozy, I discovered that quilts' geometric designs were just as beautiful to look at as they were to create. The never-ending varieties of colours, prints and patterns tickled my imagination. Traditional log cabins were my primary inspirations.

The nostalgic folklore of quilts and their place in literature initially intrigued me. As I learned more, I came to respect their place in women's history. Not only did I want to partake in this conversation of women's history, I wanted to add something new. So, I started working with salvaged wood from natural disasters to make quilts.

My wood quilts are constructed with bandsaws, chop saws, sanders and glue instead of scissors and sewing needles. Using traditional men's tools to create

wood quilts creates a harmonizing blend of masculine and feminine. Sometimes I surprise myself by how soft the wood quilts look. The artistic expression, along with the skill and technical ability needed to make a wood quilt, keeps pulling me back into the studio.

In your opinion or experience, how does the act of quilting bridge the past, present and future?

Quilts were natural vehicles for providing peace of mind, something to do with our hands and a way to create order out the chaos. American patchwork quilts are symbols of hope and are infused with meaning—political, communal, familial and personal. They have had a long history of providing comfort during times of trouble—the warmth of sleeping under grandmother's quilt during a fever, quilts made from the clothing of loved ones who have died, Quilts of Honor, quilts made to never forget those who died from AIDS... the list goes on.

Quilts can evoke so many mythologies. I love how good quilts make us feel about our past. The idea of the American pioneer woman expressing her individuality and creativity by making something out of repurposed cloth to keep her family warm is appealing. Today, many feminist artists glorify quilt making, along with other textile-based arts, as the ultimate in women's art.

I am just happy to make quilts as a form of self-expression, like so many before me have done. Because my quilts are wood and handmade, I can embrace the craft movement. Much of my wood has been collected after natural disasters, so I add to the conversation of environmental changes and concerns. My salvaged wood pieces have a bold graphic look with their use of colour that embraces abstract art. I bridge so many divides and speak many languages of fine art, craft, women's work and environmental art. It is a good place to be. ❋

“My wood quilts are constructed with bandsaws, chop saws, sanders and glue instead of scissors and sewing needles. Using traditional men’s tools to create wood quilts creates a harmonizing blend of masculine and feminine.”

WORKSPACE

Currently, my studio is a heated second-floor room above a two-car garage. One of the top three reasons my husband and I bought our home was because this room was so perfect for my work. The eastern side of the room has a view of the Atlantic Ocean. The western side has a view of hills overgrown with trees and shrubs, just perfect for birds and rabbits. The space is painted Snowfall White. Most visitors are awed by the calmness and serenity of the place. I am amazed by that because most times my studio is filled with kinetic energy, flying sawdust and frustration.

In the studio, there is a large, industrial fabric cutting table that I bought when I was a designer. That table sits in the middle of the room surrounded by two band saws—one freestanding and one tabletop—a drill press, a chop saw, a sander and a couple of dust collectors. I have one chair that I bought from a second-hand shop where I sit and sketch and journal my studio discoveries. These journals/sketchbooks are important records of mistakes, successes and ah-ha moments that help germinate more thoughts for artist statements and propel new bodies of work.

I store my wood in the garage and I rent a storage unit for the remaining collection of salvaged wood. I have collected enough wood to allow me to work for as long as I need to.

lauracheney.com
@laurapetrovichcheney

LAURA PRESTON

I am an artist, designer and business owner and I make modern minimal quilts mostly inspired by travel. I was raised in Texas and London by two architect parents, and spent several years living in New York City, where I earned a degree in art history. I met my now husband while working at a cafe in SoHo, a man who, after only a few months of dating, proposed the crazy idea of travelling around the United States for a year in his Airstream trailer. I said yes, of course, and our year-long adventure turned into over six years of living, working and travelling on the road. I discovered quilting after searching for a more practical creative outlet to do while travelling and fell in love with the craft. I launched my business, Vacilando Quilting Co., in 2015 and have been quilting full time ever since. After living nomadically for over six years, we bought a house in the Texas Hill Country in 2019 to slow down a bit and establish some deeper roots.

"Once I started travelling full time in a 200-square-foot Airstream trailer, I had to find a more practical creative outlet I could do in a small space."

What is your personal relationship or history with quilts? What draws you to them? What led you to the world of quilts?

I grew up with quilts in my home—vintage Amish quilts my grandmother collected and ones made by my great-grandmother—but never thought much of them growing up. I was always a creative kid and my mom taught me the basics of sewing, but I was very intimidated by the sewing machine. Art and craft have always fascinated me and are things I've always done in one form or another. I ended up studying art history and painting in college, and after graduating gravitated towards jobs in craft coffee and fancy cocktails. But it wasn't until a trip to Europe, in particular an afternoon watching an old Belgian woman

JOHN ELLIS, LAURA PRESTON, THE FOXES PHOTOGRAPHY

making lace by hand, that everything clicked. The idea of learning a traditional, centuries-old craft and refreshing the style to make it appealing to a younger, modern audience was really exciting to me. That idea was put on the back burner for a couple of years, but once I started travelling full time in a 200-square-foot Airstream trailer, I had to find a more practical creative outlet I could do in a small space. I discovered a few modern quilters and was really intrigued by the combination of art, utility, craft and history, so I bought some fabric and tried making a quilt. It didn't turn out great, but I was totally hooked. I've been designing and making quilts ever since.

What are your intentions when making a quilt or starting a creative project? What thought processes do you typically go through?

It's usually a long, drawn-out process that starts with a spark of inspiration—saying to myself, "Wow, that's cool!" I take a lot of photos and jot down ideas when I have them. But usually, they need to simmer for a long

while until I'm ready to start sketching them out. I like to have a pretty good idea of what the design is going to look like before I put it down on paper. Sketches usually go through many rounds of revisions and tweaks until the design feels right and feels like it captures that initial spark of inspiration. But I'm always asking myself, "How could it be better? Could it be simpler or more distilled?" I think the simplest, well-balanced designs make the biggest impact.

What mindset or attitude do you think is best for quilting? How does quilting affect your mental and physical health?

Perfection is way overrated. I say this as someone who is not a perfectionist, but one of the complaints I hear most from quilters is how their quilts aren't perfect. Handmade quilts aren't meant to be perfect—they're meant to have those little wonky imperfections that show a human made it with love. Striving for perfection will just leave you frustrated, disappointed and paralyzed.

Quilting is my job, so it comes with the stresses

"I'm a completely self-taught quilter (with the help of the Internet), so I've never really felt bound by traditional quilting conventions—mostly because I didn't know what they were!"

that any business owner would have. But then again, my job is to design and make quilts, so I can't really complain! I love being able to be creative, and quilting itself is meditative, which forces me to slow down and practice patience. Sitting and quilting all day for years does take a toll physically, so I've been doing yoga to stretch my body and keep it strong. I make sure to stretch my wrists and fingers often and try not to take on too many projects that require a lot of handwork.

Have you ever had a quilting or creative failure? What happened? What did you learn from it, if anything?

Oh absolutely! That's par for the course when running a business, especially a creative one. I've launched quilt collections I was so excited about and thought everything would sell out, only to hear crickets. I've had many months with zero sales. I've made quilts that I look back at years later and think, "What was I thinking?" I've learned that failure is part of creativity and the only thing to do about it is to keep going. Perseverance—accepting failure, figuring it out, trying again—is so important in quilting, creativity and running a business. It's when you give up that you fail.

In your opinion or experience, how does the act of quilting bridge the past, present and future?

That's my favourite part about quilting: the fact that it's a tradition and craft that people have been practising for hundreds of years and will continue to practice for decades to come. But the specialness of quilting doesn't come from the act of quilting; it comes from the emotions that a quilt stirs up. Quilts remind people

"I really love abstracting or distilling a photograph or idea down into its simplest form. And as a former art history student, I love infusing symbolism into my designs whenever I can. I've been really inspired by the natural world, bodies of water and clean architectural lines, so those have all worked their way into my work over the past couple of years."

of home, family and comfort, which is why I think they're so powerful. When I tell people I make quilts, they more often than not share a story about the quilt their great-grandmother made that they still have or the antique wedding quilt that hangs over their bed. It's something that people have their whole lives and then pass down to their kids. Few household items span generations the way a quilt does.

When and how did you become a professional?

I started my business, Vacilando Quilting Co., in February 2015 as a side hustle. After getting laid off my day job a few months later, I decided to jump in with both feet and have been quilting full time ever since.

What breadth of activity and responsibilities do you have as a professional quilter?

Most of my business is selling made-to-order quilts in my online shop, but I also take a lot of quilt commissions and collaborate with fellow artists and makers. My quilts are also carried by West Elm and a few small

online boutiques. I released my first quilt pattern in 2018 and published my first book of quilt patterns, *Simple Geometric Quilting*, in August 2019.

Are you able to support yourself in the quilt industry or do you have other endeavours as well?

Vacilando is my sole source of income. We've grown very slowly and organically, and the first couple of years weren't very financially substantial, but the last few years, as business has increased and I've been able to hire a production assistant, it's been much more stable and predictable.

What motivates and inspires you?

Becoming a better designer, artist and business motivates me. I want Vacilando to be *big*. Since the beginning, I've not-so-jokingly told my husband that he just needs to wait until I make my quilting millions. But I'm still learning how to grow a business, become a better quilter and articulate my creativity more clearly—there's no rush! I'm inspired by strong women

WORKSPACE

My husband and I share a nine-foot desk in our Airstream trailer. I have space for my Juki sewing machine and a cutting mat next to it. I have three large drawers underneath that store notions, works in progress and shipping supplies, and a basket at my feet that stores fabric. There's a ton of storage underneath our queen-size bed that stores my bolt of batting, scraps, more fabric, finished quilts and other things I don't use often. My iron and ironing board live in a closet and I usually baste smaller quilts on our small dining table.

Lately, I've been doing less quilt production to focus more on running the business, so my production assistant, Lindsay, has taken on more quilt making in her home studio in Ohio.

Soon I'll be moving my studio into one of the spare bedrooms in the house my husband and I are renovating in the Texas Hill Country. I'm not quite sure what I'll do with all that space, but it'll definitely be nice to spread out a bit.

making names for themselves, and artists and designers who understand and express their vision with the world, and I'm always inspired by the natural world around me.

Do any particular ideas, objects or activities—outside of and unrelated to quilting—inform and inspire your quilting practice?

I'm really inspired by other artistic mediums—painting, ceramics, garments, sculpture, architecture. Twentieth-century art, especially abstract expressionism, Bauhaus, minimalism and really any work done around the middle of the century have inspired a lot of my work. After travelling full time and living minimally in the Airstream trailer my husband and I designed and built, both travel and minimalism fuel my practice and my aesthetic. ✻

vacilandoquilting.co
@vacilandoquilting

Moderation

Moderation

by **LeeAnn Decker**

When you first glance at this quilt, "moderation" might not be the first word that comes to mind. But the process of designing it was all about that! It started, as many of my quilts do, with a box of orphan blocks—pre-made pieces that didn't find their homes in other quilts. I love to work this way and have made several quilts from my box of orphans.

First, I grab a bunch of blocks I want to use and drop them on the floor, noticing how the colours and patterns go together. Next, I place them on the design wall and see what fits together by measurement—same size blocks together. I work quickly, get a bunch of blocks on the wall, and stand back to see what's developing.

Then I discover the blocks that "don't play well with others." I shoot photos on my phone as I go along, and transform them into black-and-white so that the values of the colours become apparent. No matter how attached I am to using certain blocks, I have to let them go if the value isn't right.

I had made the block that spells "moderation" several years ago, using instructions in the book *Word Play Quilts* by Tonya Ricucci (Martingale, 2010). As moderation is always a good thing to develop in life, I decided to think about the concept as I designed this quilt. Some synonyms for moderation are calmness, patience, restraint and balance. I tried to bring those qualities into this quilt, using the blocks and fabrics I had on hand. Most of the blocks are made from scraps of old clothing, and I bought nothing to complete the quilt. I strived for calm colours, restraint in value, symmetrical balance and a lot of patience. Making this quilt was definitely a practice in moderation!

It was professionally quilted by Sharon Tucker. ❄

niftyquilts.com
@niftyquilts

LAURIE RUSSMAN

I am a fibre artist who creates unique textile art inspired by photographs. Brilliant colour and playful kitties are the hallmarks of my work. My other day job keeps me on the road and you can always find me taking strange pictures of ordinary objects that can be transformed into magical inspiration for neon-hued travel scenes.

I began teaching quilting where I learned my craft—at the beloved but no longer open City Quilter in NYC. This grew into lots of Open Studios sessions at the International Quilt Festival and appearances on *Quilting Arts TV* on PBS.

I also love to write about the creative process and am a frequent contributor to *Quilting Arts* magazine (I have also written for *Canadian Quilter* and *Art Quilting Studio*). My quilts have been juried into International Quilt Festival in Houston, AQS QuiltWeek in Paducah and the National Juried Show at Quilt Canada.

My husband and I live in a tree-laden small town in Connecticut with three mischievous felines and a tall, handsome German Shepherd named Kane—as well as many furry and feathered "tenants" who make their home near our house. As a former city kid, I find myself in a constant state of wonder; in one recent morning, our front lawn featured a hawk, baby rabbit and bobcat (none of whom ate one another, fortunately).

"I am an art quilter. My work is very representational (down to the last whisker), with raw-edged fusible appliqué, lots of stitching and texture."

What is your personal relationship or history with quilts? What draws you to them? What led you to the world of quilts?

My path began with the project my husband drily titled The Guilt Quilt—a hand-pieced, hand-quilted doll quilt for my daughter, created *very* slowly during lots of business trips. My guilty working-mother-self decided that her American Girl doll must have a quilt

and entered the magical place formerly known as the City Quilter in NYC. The colour! The texture! As I ran my fingers across the bolts of fabric, the memories of my mother teaching me to sew garments came flooding back. Simple, functional quilts were my apprenticeship; I figured that a solid base in the fundamentals was the best place to begin.

The other magical moment, and the one that truly ignited my passion for art quilting, was an email from Houston informing me that my quilt Neon Kitty had been accepted into a special exhibit at International Quilt Festival. I had discovered art quilting and loved it, but this external affirmation inspired me to commit myself.

What are your intentions when making a quilt or starting a creative project? What thought processes do you typically go through?

If my subject is a dog or a cat, my objective is to create a piece that captures the spirit of that pet: soulful, playful, disdainful (that would be for cats) and simply adorable. This is an emotional process... invariably I fall in love with my subject by the time I finish the portrait.

For landscapes and travel scenes and still lifes, I work to distill the scene down to the most important details, impressions and colours, hoping to encourage the viewer to see things in a different way.

What mindset or attitude do you think is best for quilting? How does quilting affect your mental and physical health?

My mantra: make what you love. The more art you make, the more likely it will please others—your joy of making it will be palpable.

How? First, be fearless! Cut into that fabric, try that acrylic ink... keep going. The quilt will tell you what you need to do next if you listen. I rarely know how I will actually quilt a piece once it is completely fused and ready for my machine; I simply begin with one section I am sure about and figure it out as I go.

Next, submit your work! As my mother used to say, what is the worst that can happen? Share the joy of your art and view your inevitable rejection-note pile as a sign that you are trying.

Also very important: quilting is not a contest and not a zero-sum game. Be happy for the success of others and promote their work! This is a very small community of amazingly gifted artists who, in my experience, love to help others who are in earlier stages of their craft. I am incredibly grateful to my friends who helped me and love to coach new members of our tribe.

What quilt traditions do you hold dear? What quilting conventions do you ignore or challenge?

The best tradition is the sense of community and belief that a quilt can help heal. My most meaningful projects have been group quilts stitched together to express love and support for a friend battling illness. A sense of joy permeates the process, from the communication and organization to the anticipation of how much it will mean to our friend.

WORKSPACE

Ah, room of my heart! When we moved to our current house, I took half of the loft as my studio.

It is not large but it is open on two sides to the rest of the house and its current design makes use of every inch (pitched ceilings can be a challenge, so I have an enormous sewing table tucked into that side of the room). Built-in shelves house my fabric, Singer Featherweights (my mom and aunt are the friendly ghosts here) and my UPPERCASE magazine collection. My blog posts about how my husband and I designed it are the best-read pieces on my site. I love pretty much everything about it, including the large dog bed tucked under my cutting table for my loyal studio assistant.

What breadth of activity and responsibilities do you have as a professional quilter?

My work encompasses commissions for pet portraits, teaching classes, writing articles for quilting publications and creating designs for Windham Fabrics.

Are you able to support yourself in the quilt industry or do you have other endeavours as well?

My life is in a transition stage: still in financial services, increasingly in the quilt world. When I retire, I plan to ramp up my teaching schedule, as well as every other aspect of my creative work. I can't wait! ✻

"As an art quilter, there really aren't very many conventions to follow. I do stick with two-dimensional quilts, layered with batting and backing, but from that point on, anything goes. Which is, after all, the joy of art quilting!"

neonkittyquilts.com
@neonkittyquilts

MADAY DELGADO

As an art educator living in the Midwest, I'm passionate about sustainability and urban gardening, and committed to maintaining a public garden space in the downtown area where I reside with my family. I spent my formative years living in Cuba, where I was born, and migrated to the USA as a teen, settling in NYC in the 1990s. My professional background is in the banking industry. I switched careers over five years ago and now lead workshops in a variety of mediums while working full time.

In all workshops, I encourage sustainability as a way to build confidence and community, with a back-to-basics approach and awareness about resource use and waste. I focus on the perfectly imperfect aspects of discovery by exploring new tools and techniques, and leading workshops from painting, weaving and printing to quilting by hand and machine. I believe that creating with purpose and intention, and guiding others to embrace their individual creative paths, is the starting point to a transformative and healing future, personally and collectively.

PORTRAIT BY KARMEN LINDNER PHOTOGRAPHY

"My studio is the lab where I learn, adapt and create."

What is your personal relationship or history with quilts? What draws you to them? What led you to the world of quilts?

I had a simple goal when I discovered sewing after my child was born; to create collages with fabric instead of the traditional scrapbooking with paper. After my baby was born, I desperately needed to find something that belonged to me, at least in my new role

as a mother and living in a small town I had moved to five short years before. I loved to paint, but it took too long to set up with a small child.

One Saturday morning, while going for a walk with my toddler, I stumbled upon a local sewing shop. After looking around, I decided that I would buy a sewing machine. I had never, ever sewn by machine. I returned within a few days and purchased what would become one of many sewing machines. The more I learned about sewing, the more I wanted to do it, all of the time. I never considered myself a quilter, but quilts are some of the items that I truly enjoy completing and teaching others about.

In my 10th year of sewing, traditions and storytelling are what continue to draw me infinitely to the world of sewing. A perfect day for me starts with a workshop and getting to meet like-minded people, interested in forging connections and working together to make our lives better with creativity.

How would you describe your style or aesthetic?

I consider myself a lover of chaotic beauty, always questioning and seeking; others may say that "free spirit" is a better descriptor.

I live to create work that pushes the boundaries of materials, colour, texture and passion for one's work. I try to communicate that to my students. Ultimately I create my work improvisationally. I always share my work in a workshop format and let the students decide if the technique I used speaks to them as much as it did to me. Often, it does.

What are your intentions when making a quilt or starting a creative project? What thought processes do you typically go through?

There are times when I start a project because a customer or friend expressed an interest in a specific technique; other times I'm inspired by a fabric line, a photo, an abstract idea, my gardens or something from my childhood. Almost always, an idea is accompanied by a workshop proposal. I'm always wondering about the best way of presenting a workshop because teaching is what inspires me the most. That brings me to people: I love to be in the company of creatives because I learn from them as much as or perhaps more than they learn from me.

I don't wish to create to hide my work in the basement. I create with the idea that others will critique it, love it or even hate it. I thrive in my work because I'm curious and I want to share it so perhaps others can see that there is nothing impossible or daunting in the act of sewing; in fact, the more daunting it seems, the more drawn I am to it. I'm passionate about sharing my creative world, and if the opportunity arose, I would probably walk down the street like a sewing prophet, door to door (or maybe just sit in the corner with a sign).

What mindset or attitude do you think is best for quilting? How does quilting affect your mental and physical health?

Sewing is peace, freedom, healing, supportive and, mostly for me, my spiritual practice. Sewing is helping me combat difficult childhood memories, and work through the loneliness of living in a place I'm working to love and accept after many years. Whether by hand or machine, sewing sparks joy and a feeling of having arrived "home."

Having an open mind, welcoming happy accidents (or what others call mistakes) is a must when trying something new. If the idea of creating something big is frightening, start with something small. Take a class or two, read books or magazines, but please, stay away from YouTube whenever possible. There are so many resources that support working artists and visionaries.

"I believe that everyone can be creative in any medium they choose at any time. Let's not be defined by the label 'artist.' It can be an overwhelming and limiting adjective, as well as intimidating.

For me, the primordial role of creativity is to take us outside of the mundane, everyday activities, and to help us heal.

Art, in any form you choose, is here to lift, challenge and educate us. All of us have it inside of ourselves. Let's exalt others' abilities and create such excitement that they too will want to try it. Art lives and breathes with us."

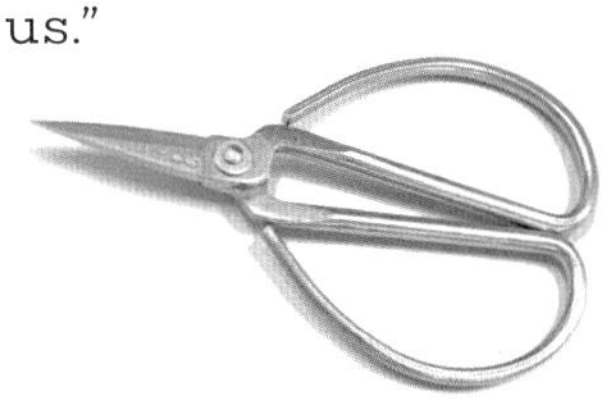

Find a local business that welcomes and supports you. Most importantly, just start—do anything you like and do it *your way* because yours will be more gratifying in the long run.

What quilt traditions do you hold dear? What quilting conventions do you ignore or challenge?

I'm deeply in love with Japanese sashiko hand stitching and boro techniques, and have been since early 2016. I began leading workshops following this aesthetic in 2017 with the launch of the Midwest Fiber Arts Trails, a network of makers focused on community and education. When I began to teach sashiko, I encountered disbelief that the technique would stick; hand stitching simply took too long. Shops nearby were not selling supplies yet, but soon curiosity surfaced and it was embraced.

I consider mending and upcycling materials to be a gift to ourselves and the environment in the long run. The idea of using garments, fabrics and other items passed down from generation to generation brings me joy. I did not have sewing in my life growing up or traditions that got passed down to me—perhaps I was too young to remember. There is something incredibly beautiful about honouring textile traditions and items that belonged to those no longer here with us. Quilting with the discarded is alluring, and it inspires me to preserve and not waste. Resource conservation is always my goal.

I don't follow national quilting conventions because they seem too far away from where I live. I hope that conventions continue to inspire and promote diversity in the creative process and in the support of teachers from different parts of the world, leading creative lives wherever we are planted. The key to any sustainable and creative pursuit is collaboration and diversity of people and ideas.

no chasing
No
cleverly
explained
dilemmas
PEACE
FOR
STAND
MORGAN
made
the design
protest
universal
revered virgen
WEST
EAST
NYC

"There is nothing more beautiful to me than the unique markings derived from a hand stitch; I'm humbled by the hard work and preparation, even the dedication of those who lived before us, because making do is a universal truth and not a romantic musing."

In your opinion or experience, how does the act of quilting bridge the past, present and future?

Traditions. One of the reasons I love hand stitching and quilting is the ability to communicate or tell stories both from the present and the past and to share with one another in a quieter setting. We hear the longing in each other's stories—stories about grandmothers and great-grandmothers from around the world. We know from these stories how hard they worked to provide, care and mend.

We can hear each other without the noise of a sewing machine; we can connect to a past and reminisce about how things used to get done. I'm intrigued by the time and effort that our ancestors—no matter what part of the world we are from—spent working by hand, after the day's work was done, infusing life back into a garment, a sheet or a bedspread. I long for that connection to those people I have never met but with whom I feel so intimately attached because of their struggles, their triumphs and their make-do attitudes.

When we have no choice or when resources are lacking, necessity forces us to be creative and innovative; I want that connection and aspire to forge a community of like-minded creatives, friends, customers and students, who promote well-being and cooperation by creating and being with one another.

What breadth of activity and responsibilities do you have as a professional quilter?

I'm a textile artist and teacher leading workshops at shops, galleries and most recently the local university, teaching children. I present at quilt guilds, partake in community-building events in and outside of my home state, and support nonprofits that spearhead fibre art education and community initiatives such as libraries by donating new sewing machines.

WORKSPACE

My home studio is located in the basement. It's a large space that accommodates weaving looms, sewing machines, workstations for painting and tables on wheels. I love that I can leave projects in different stages of completion and no one can see the perfectly chaotic mess. I also have plenty of room to hang smaller hand-stitched pieces that continue to inspire me and provide a colourful backdrop to an otherwise sunless room.

Are you able to support yourself in the quilt industry or do you have other endeavours as well?

I work full time at a local sewing shop, where I teach regularly during shop hours and after hours. I have decided that I enjoy sewing so much, I want to continue loving it instead of making it the sole source of income for myself and my family.

What motivates and inspires you?

Creating an inclusive, artistic platform across generations, for all, while promoting a sustainable future is just as powerful a motivator as my family. Meeting new people and sharing with each other what we love is also an important part of my journey. I hope that the work I create makes a difference in people's lives, that it brings them joy, inspires their curiosity or draws them closer to their artistic realization, as they adopt my suggestions or create new ones that challenge them, as much as mine invigorate me.

Do any particular ideas, objects or activities—outside of and unrelated to quilting—inform and inspire your quilting practice?

I love vintage items, though I admit I do not like a cluttered home so I don't collect a lot of things except fabrics and art supplies!

I enjoy sharing what I have with others, from dinners to plants, to household items, and working in my gardens, volunteer or home-based ones. When I'm not working outside during the warm months, I love painting my house to add decorative touches and discovering new places with my family. ❇

sustainabletextiledesign.com
@sustainabletextiledesign

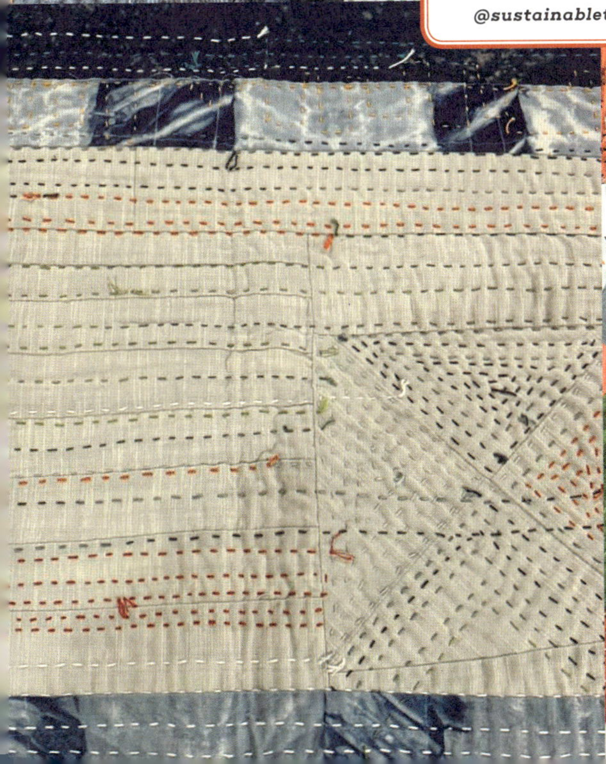

Crazy Quilt

by **Elizabeth Duke**

I hand and machine sew garments, home décor and journals. Inspiration and materials often come from acquired and cherished antique quilts and fabrics. This vintage crazy quilt hung for years in a family friend's home. My mom, who knew how I admired the quilt, purchased it for me. It now proudly hangs in my home.

The quilt blocks are made from fabric scraps and memorabilia, and dates stitched into threadbare sections go back to 1837. It appears that many hands were at work stitching and piecing the quilt top together. There's a gentle unevenness in its construction.

This crazy quilt inspired the making of a crazy vest and skirt. Just like this quilt, my garments include vintage elements of fabric bits (velvets, silks, cottons) and fibres (floss, perle cotton, silk thread and ribbon), as well as charms and beads. This love for vintage textiles and haberdashery traces back to my childhood. The women in my family—my mother, grandmother and aunts—always had a keen eye for identifying, collecting, displaying and caring for linens. I have tremendous gratitude for the textile and family history they've taught and shared. With this reverence and knowledge, I mindfully select and incorporate vintage cloths, threads and embellishments into my pieces. While working on a garment, I wonder about the stitchers of yore. What were their processes and intents: utility, pleasure, ceremony, legacy? I will probably never uncover the answers, yet I love imagining possible scenarios and reasons! ❇

edukedesigns.wordpress.com
@sewistt44

MALKA DUBRAWSKY

I am an artist and designer, but most importantly a maker. I've been primarily a maker of textiles, having gotten a bachelor of fine arts in studio art about 30 years ago. Though my focus then was in printmaking, my exploration quickly turned to dyeing and patterning fabric, as well as creating with that handmade cloth. Over the years, I've designed fabric, written books and articles, taught workshops and sold my handcrafted goods both at quilt and craft shows and online.

What is your personal relationship or history with quilts? What draws you to them? What led you to the world of quilts?

Though I've been making quilts for decades, I don't have a family history with quilts or even early memories of them. I was originally drawn to them because, having completed an art degree, I began a series of drawings that reminded me of my own vague notion of what a quilt was and wanted to translate that from paper to fabric.

"My quilts are designed with basic shapes and are meant to read as single images rather than a collection of blocks. Moving the eye across the surface, particularly controlling that movement, is important in my work."

What are your intentions when making a quilt or starting a creative project? What thought processes do you typically go through?

I'm always building on an exploration leftover from a previous piece. No one quilt answers all my "what if" questions, so that's often the basis for the next design.

Also, every quilt has to have a function, at least in my own mind. It may never be a bed quilt or a baby quilt, but I spend some time imagining its purpose.

"I'm drawn to quilts because they're accessible, and no matter how intricate or art-like, quilts carry an aura of functionality and that speaks to me."

What mindset or attitude do you think is best for quilting? How does quilting affect your mental and physical health?

A mind open to possibilities is best for quilting—though I think it's more about trusting yourself. Every quilt is a design problem, and you have to believe that, somehow, you'll find your way to the answer.

Have you ever had a quilting or creative failure? What happened? What did you learn from it, if anything?

Absolutely, all the time. You can't have success without failure or you'd never grow artistically. You have to know what you don't like, to know what you do like. When something doesn't work out, I let myself feel disappointed and then ask myself if there's something in this failure that I do like, something that can be the seed of a new idea.

What quilt traditions do you hold dear? What quilting conventions do you ignore or challenge?

I love old quilts, particularly simple quilts and Amish quilts. I love that they were made to adhere to very specific guidelines, with materials at hand and truly crafted with precision. I ignore any convention, quilting or otherwise, that tells me I have to make something a specific way or it's not done right. Though I love cats, I'm very fond of the saying, "There's more than one way to skin that cat."

How does the act of quilting bridge the past, present and future?

Putting bits of fabric together to make something functional is a pretty ancient activity. Wanting to enhance those sewn bits, either through embellishment or by making definitive choices about which bits are used and how they're sewn together, is potentially one of the things that makes us human. If that doesn't link us through the generations, I'm not sure what does.

When did you become a professional?

I've always seen myself as a professional and approached my work that way. To that end, selling my work or the auxiliary knowledge I've gained in making that work has and is a consideration. My professional motto is "pursue every opportunity," and I've functioned within that ideal to get teaching gigs, book contracts, magazine exposure and design jobs.

What breadth of activity and responsibilities do you have as a professional quilter?

I do everything from dyeing and patterning fabric to designing quilts, illustrating and crafting my patterns, as well as teaching workshops and vending at quilt and craft shows. The only aspect of my business I outsource is tech editing and quilting.

Are you able to support yourself in the quilt industry or do you have other endeavours as well?

No. Designing, crafting, teaching, pattern writing and selling are not enough financially. I have a couple of other side gigs that make the work possible and they are totally worth it.

WORKSPACE

I work out of my house, where I have two dedicated areas. I do all my dye and fabric patterning work in my garage, and my sewing and computer-oriented work in a spare room. I'm very lucky to have that much space to explore my ideas.

What motivates and inspires you?

As simple and possibly pedantic as this sounds, I really like making things, especially functional things. The joke at my house is that my hobby is also sewing, as I love sewing clothes, particularly for myself, and will often dye cotton for a quilt in the same dye bath I've created to colour a length of linen for a future garment.

If I craft things for personal use, both for myself and others, I'm living a bit more intentionally.

Do any particular ideas, objects or activities—outside of and unrelated to quilting—inform and inspire your quilting practice?

I've been athletic for the entirety of my adult life. I spent 15 years swimming on a competitive swim team and have run marathons and half marathons and trail races. I even ran across the Grand Canyon in 2016.

Lately I've noticed, though it's always been there, that movement is a big theme in my work. I use simple forms, colour and value changes to move the viewer's eye across a quilted surface. ❋

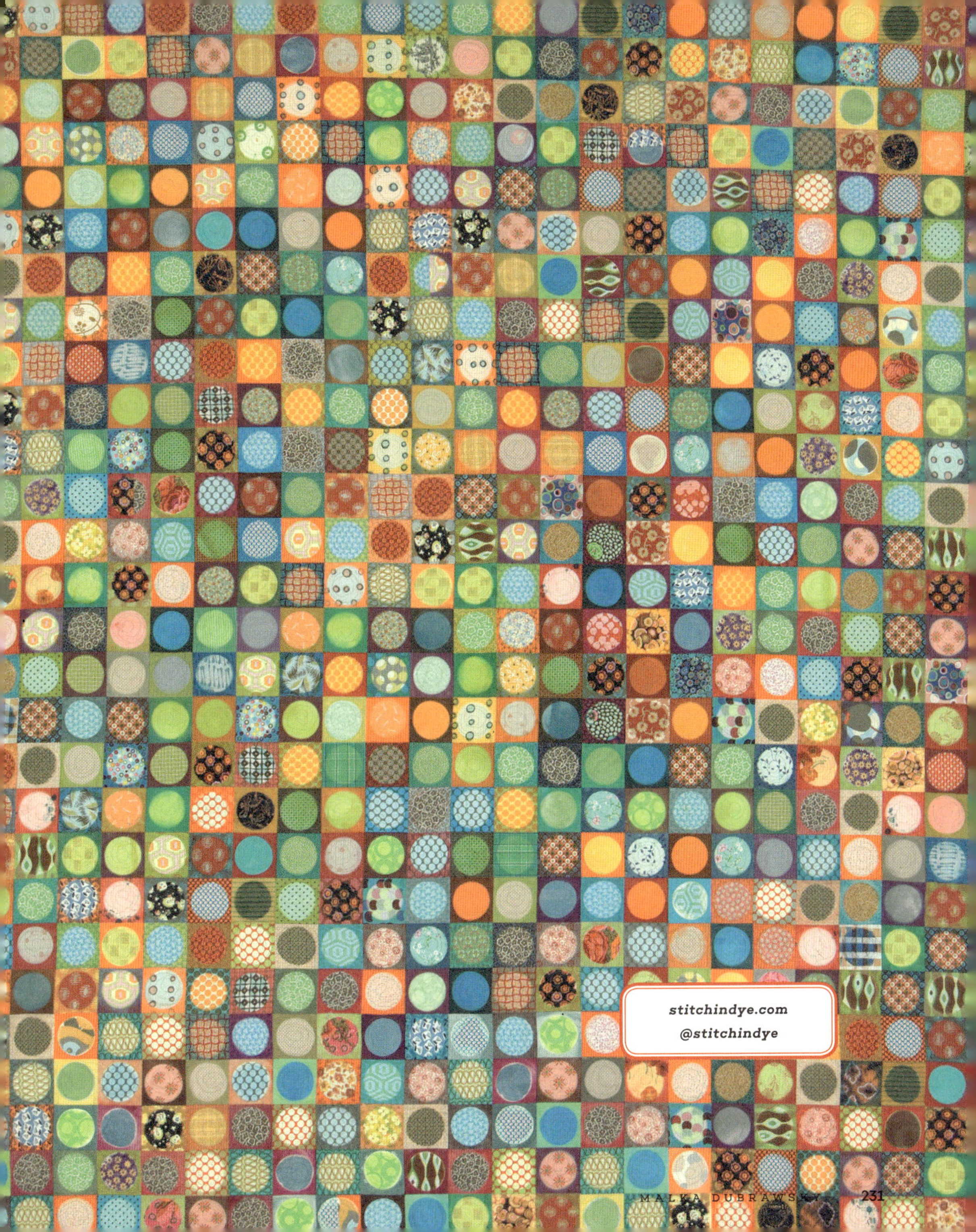

stitchindye.com
@stitchindye

MARYLINE COLLIOUD -ROBERT

I am a Swiss quilter and teacher. I've been making quilts for 45 years and I still enjoy doing so, just as much as on the first day! I have three grown-up children and several grandchildren. I mostly make contemporary quilts. I exhibit my quilts in international exhibitions and I teach all over Europe. I've started a line of quilting patterns on Etsy. I have bought hundreds of fabrics over the years and always dive into my drawers to make a quilt. I don't buy fabrics anymore, or very rarely.

"Piecing, sewing and making colour interactions mean everything to me. I've been doing that for so long I can't imagine ever stopping. I lose track of time and I lose myself in the fabrics. It's not a choice, it's a must."

What is your personal relationship or history with quilts? What draws you to them? What led you to the world of quilts?

I was an exchange student in California when I was 18 and slept under a quilt for a year. Nobody made quilts in my new American family, but still, I picked it up somehow, as I started to make patchwork quilts as soon as I got back home. I taught myself with books and magazines. I started with one or two traditional blocks but soon made my own designs, as there was no quilting tradition or patchwork examples in my country. I haven't stopped since!

How would you describe your style or aesthetic?

I make intensely coloured surfaces, either pieced, appliquéd or reverse appliquéd. I look for colour interactions and I play with multicoloured shapes. I'm

fascinated by minimalist and quiet quilts, but can't make any in such a style. I always add more and more colours! My quilts are somehow traditional in the making, as they have three layers, quilted mostly by machine, but the upper surface is contemporary, as it doesn't use any traditional blocks. I usually make quite large wall quilts.

What are your intentions when making a quilt or starting a creative project? What thought processes do you typically go through?

My first inspiration is always colour. I usually have some colour combination or gradation or harmony to start with, and I begin collecting all the fabrics I'll use to make the quilt. This process of working on colour choices can take several days. I pile and arrange dozens, sometimes hundreds of fabrics until I have a satisfying feeling of completion. Only then do I start to sew.

I'm a very visual person and I'm always taking pictures when I'm outside. I used to write complicated colour descriptions in a small notebook when I found some interesting composition, but now, thanks to a smartphone, I can instantly document my findings.

What mindset or attitude do you think is best for quilting? How does quilting affect your mental and physical health?

I can put myself into a creative mood instantly. I was already making quilts before I had children and once they were here, sometimes I only had 10 minutes a day to make something, so it was good training!

I must say that I have never lacked ideas for my quilts. I literally have drawers full of projects I'll never have time to make in my lifetime. And there are always new ones jumping in! But I've noticed that the best way to develop new ideas or to find new energy is to start a project—anything. Just by making something, new ideas will start pouring in.

What quilt traditions do you hold dear? What quilting conventions do you ignore or challenge?

I'm fascinated by traditional quilts, and if I were rich, I would be an avid collector of antique quilts. I love the repetition of the blocks. It provides a structure and a rhythm that makes me feel good. I especially love scraps and string quilts. I love the way some quilters reached such a high level of design with tiny leftovers. I've been quilting for so long—I have tons of scraps and I use them a lot in my work.

In your opinion or experience, how does the act of quilting bridge the past, present and future?

I'm part of an immense movement of women who did things with their hands and created something aesthetic with them. I'm in awe of how humanity has always tried to make everyday objects prettier or better looking than strictly necessary for their use. Fabric is less intimidating than oil painting, for example, and it allows so many people to express themselves in creative ways.

WORKSPACE

I'm working in my home and I'm lucky to have a whole (messy!) room to myself. I have a large pin wall, a small table for my sewing machine, a larger table for cutting (and which also works as an office desk, and is therefore overloaded with everything that shouldn't be there) and a large chest of drawers with hundreds of fabrics sorted by colour and style.

I love my studio and the fact that everything is close by. I have to tidy, sort and make room before starting every new quilt, but I like the process. I think about the quilt to be made and I enjoy handling all my material and putting it into place. I sort the fabric by colour and I put them back in the drawers, before probably pulling them out soon for the new project.

Would you consider yourself as a professional within the quilting industry? When and how did you become a professional?

I started teaching locally, and it spread from there to magazine articles, international teaching and exhibiting. I teach classes in several countries, mostly on the subject of quilting and colour interactions. I created some patterns, as I love teaching. It gives me the opportunity to teach from home, without the hassle of being on the road all the time.

Are you able to support yourself in the quilt industry or do you have other endeavours as well?

I used to teach French as a foreign language in an international hotel management school. I'm now retired. I don't support myself through quilting. I'd say that what I make covers the cost of fabrics, books, materials and travel expenses to quilt shows and such.

What motivates and inspires you?

I wake up every morning looking forward to being in my studio, and to sewing, even if sometimes only for short moments. I find inspiration around me, mostly from nature, travelling, old walls, peeling paints, but always from all the unexpected colour combinations I stumble upon. ❋

marylinecollioudrobert.com
@mary_and_patch

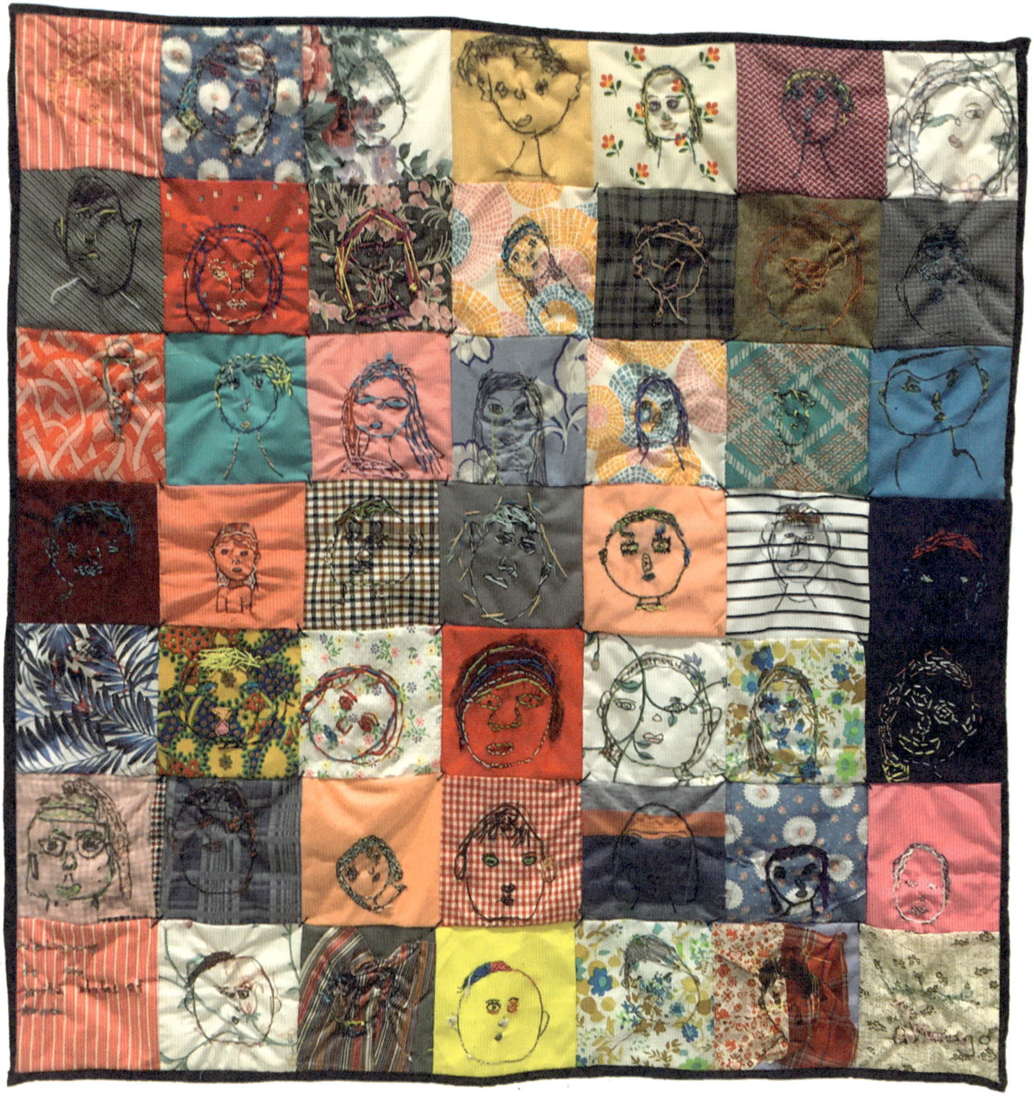

Welcome Blanket

by **Jayna Zweiman**

"All are welcome to get involved in positive, proactive, civic-based art making."

The Welcome Blanket Project aims to connect people already living in the United States with our country's newest immigrants through stories and handmade blankets, providing both symbolic and literal comfort and warmth. At the same time, the project offers a positive, hands-on way to understand the scope of a 2,000-mile proposed border wall and to subvert it from an idea of exclusion to one of inclusion. By participating in this project, people come together to talk about immigration policy and how it affects real people.

Makers quilt, knit, crochet, weave and sew welcome blankets. The design guidelines are simply that it be 40 inches square and easy to care for—and be something you love so much it is hard to give away. With each welcome blanket, makers are invited to share stories important to their families about immigration, migration and relocation.

The quilt shown here is an example of how an innovative educator used a welcome blanket as the basis for discussing the history of crafting and immigration. Art teacher Allison Beaulieu Cholke developed a learning unit at the University of Chicago Lab School that included this concept of aggregate self-portraits for her third-grade classes. With the group welcome blankets, students included notes of welcome for new immigrants coming to the United States.

Welcome Blanket has been hosted at the Smart Museum of Art (Chicago, Illinois), MODA (Museum of Design Atlanta, in Atlanta, Georgia) and Fuller Craft Museum (Brockton, Massachusetts), with more exhibitions planned. Over 5,000 welcome blanket gifts have been created, displayed and distributed through our refugee resettlement partners. ✻

welcomeblanket.org
@welcomeblanket

NADRA RIDGEWAY

I am a professional fabric and pattern designer, quiltmaker and teacher in Germany. I have designed several fabric lines for the quilting and home sewing industry, I run an Etsy shop where I sell PDF quilt patterns and I teach quiltmaking in fabric shops around the country.

It was in the early 2000s when I first discovered American craft and quilting blogs on the Internet. I fell in love with all the beautiful craft projects and the colourful fabrics, which I had never seen before. I was especially drawn to the whimsical 1930s reproduction prints and their beautiful colours—prints like these just weren't available in Germany and I clearly remember the first times I ordered quilting fabric from overseas, which was quite an adventure. Sometimes I had to wait for weeks and weeks until they arrived.

This new world of craft blogging really fascinated me and I soon started my own blog, where I shared small patchwork projects I made from free tutorials and the first patterns designed by myself. One of my first quilts was a baby quilt for my son, which I made with help from quilters I met on a virtual quilting bee.

How would you describe your style or aesthetic?

My quilts are colourful and bright. I often use traditional patterns, which I try to give a modern twist by using contemporary fabrics and colours or modifying the quilt layouts. I am drawn to small-scale prints, which I combine with pastel solids or low-volume prints. Sometimes I use embellishments or combine

"Quilting is my creative voice and it feeds my soul; it's meditative and relaxing. I love working with beautiful fabrics and colours, and learning new techniques. Seeing a project develop from start to finish and connecting with like-minded people brings me the most joy."

traditional piecing with appliqué to underline a characteristic element of the pattern, and I love to finish off projects with a few hand-quilting stitches for the extra personal touch.

Colour plays a huge role for me. I mostly work with harmonious colour schemes and put a lot of emphasis on finding perfectly matching prints. I gravitate towards primary colours but also love working with less popular colours like orange, brown or purple. There are no ugly colours—in my opinion, it's all about the coordinating prints that can build a connection between allegedly mismatched colours.

What are your intentions when making a quilt or starting a creative project? What thought processes do you typically go through?

Personally, I make quilts and patchwork projects for family and friends. As a professional, I create patterns for quilt enthusiasts around the world. When creating quilt patterns my intentions are focused on my customers: I want them to be able to create a beautiful project and have the best possible experience—beginners and experienced quilters alike. I really enjoy the creative process of coming up with fun pattern ideas that can be incorporated into different projects. But the technical side is just as important: taking the guesswork out of the process by using easy piecing methods, eliminating needless steps and creating easy-to-understand instructions are my main goals.

What mindset or attitude do you think is best for quilting? How does quilting affect your mental and physical health?

When starting out it's helpful to be curious and open to experimentation. There are many ways to make a quilt, and it might take a while to find the preferred way or technique. It might also be helpful to adjust high expectations and set aside perfectionism in order

to find joy in the process. It's easy to feel dissatisfied with aspects of your quilting (the colour choices or accuracy of piecing for example), but this shouldn't keep you from finishing a project.

I was reminded of my own struggle with perfectionism just recently: a few years ago I made a mini quilt and after having finished the last quilting line I realized that I'd misplaced the blocks. I never completed the project and found it on a stack of UFOs (unfinished objects) a few weeks ago. When I look at this wonderful little project I can't even tell now what had bothered me back then.

Have you ever had a quilting or creative failure? What happened? What did you learn from it, if anything?

Several years ago I created an Alphabet quilt pattern and made a sample for my son's bedroom. It was a lot of work and we both really loved this quilt. The colourful letters beautifully popped against a white background. The backing fabric was a fiery red print with little white stars—the perfect combination. One day the quilt got wet and the colour bled through the quilt top. Since then I'm very careful with vibrant dyes and use colour catchers when washing my quilts.

Other than that I have made many smaller and bigger mistakes along the way, but I don't consider them as failures. I have made it a habit to read instructions from start to finish, measure twice, clear my sewing table before I start cutting fabric and keep my coffee mug out of reach.

What quilt traditions do you hold dear? What quilting conventions do you ignore or challenge?

I have tried several different quilting techniques but I always come back to traditional machine piecing. I never prewash but always spray starch my fabric before cutting and I spray baste and machine bind my quilts. I don't think quiltmaking has to follow any particular rules. For me, it's all about enjoying the process and end results, and stressing less about the perfect or right way to get there.

In your opinion or experience, how does the act of quilting bridge the past, present and future?

Like any other craft, quilting is a tradition passed down through generations. They're often passed down as heirlooms through generations of family members. I am the first quilter in my family but my mother is an avid crafter who taught me how to sew, knit and crochet. Growing up in a creative household has strongly influenced my quilting journey.

Today, my son keeps me company in my studio. He follows my work while being on his own creative journey. A few years ago he asked me if he could design a quilt block for me to turn into a quilt for him. I gave him detailed instructions on how to draw his design and he came up with a little robot named Lori! I turned the drawing into a pattern and made a quilt for his room, which is hanging on the wall right beside his desk. Maybe someday he'll decorate the room of his child with this robot quilt we made. And maybe someday he'll teach his child how to quilt.

When and how did you become a professional?

After high school, I went to university for media studies and worked in a media agency for several years. I have always loved to craft, and making handmade gifts for friends and family just felt natural. My career as a professional quilter started with a handmade gift for a newborn baby. The rattle toys I made were really popular, and gradually the creation of other accessories built the foundation for a whole collection. During parental leave, I founded my label ellis & higgs and started selling handmade items. After moving to the

countryside I opened a shop and studio in our courtyard, which I ran for two years. Today it serves as a second studio space—I decided to quit the labour-intensive production of custom-made items and instead focus on my design work.

Working with beautiful quilting fabrics soon triggered the wish to create my own designs. With the help of a friend, I learned to turn my drawings into digital files. After taking my first steps on Spoonflower, I sent my portfolio to one of the big fabric companies. I have created four fabric collections for Riley Blake Designs. At the same time, I started designing quilt patterns to highlight my fabric collections. Today I've sold more than 100 PDF quilt patterns in my Etsy shop. Quilting has been a side business for a long time, but in 2016 I decided to leave the corporate world and become a full-time quilter. I've never looked back.

What motivates and inspires you?

I am motivated by the joy I feel whilst being creative and the joy of others who were either gifted a quilt I made or who made a project from one of my patterns. I love it when customers get in touch to tell me that they've just made their very first quilt or when they proudly send a picture of their finished project.

Do any particular ideas, objects or activities—outside of and unrelated to quilting—inform and inspire your quilting practice?

I am mainly inspired by my surroundings: my house and garden, my neighbourhood and everyday objects. My patterns are based on specific topics like seasonal events and activities that we encounter in everyday life, and which don't necessarily have anything to do with quilting. I also draw a lot of inspiration from crafting alongside my son. I often ask for his opinion when designing my quilt block motifs and I really appreciate his advice. He has such a different perspective and makes the best suggestions when it comes to unique details. ❄

WORKSPACE

I live and work on a renovated farm in a small village near my hometown of Frankfurt, Germany, together with my family. Our house is an old cow shed that was turned into a timber-framed family home. My studio is a bright and airy room with lots of space, and roof windows orientated to the southern side. The wooden beams on the walls and ceiling tell stories from the past. I arranged my studio entirely to my taste and needs: simple and minimalist with white furniture and only a few colourful accessories. A modern black carpet on the floor is a statement piece that builds a beautiful contrast. My studio is my happy place—I love spending time here all day!

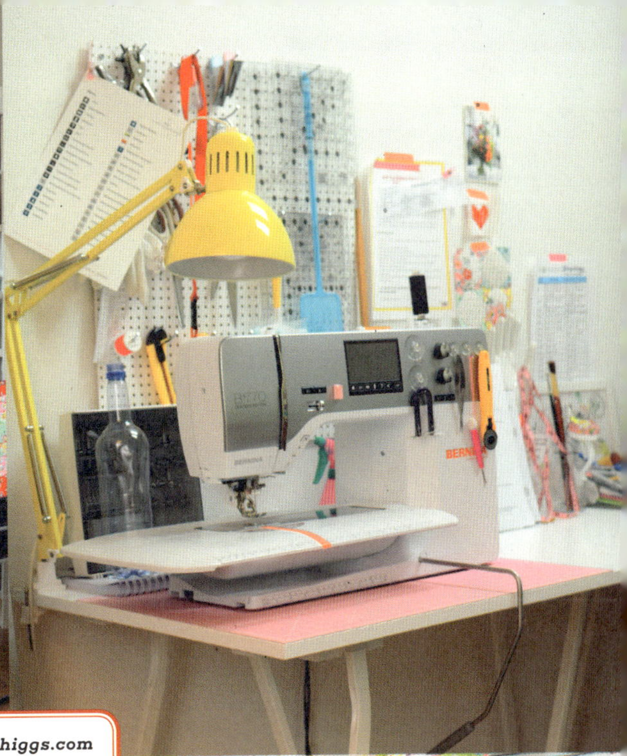

ellisandhiggs.com
@ellisandhiggs

NANCY PURVIS

On the surface, one would see me as a published quilter and artist living the life in Raleigh, North Carolina, with my husband and two children. I am your average mother juggling life and family, and most days am exhausted by 8pm. I enjoy weight lifting, getting outdoors, exploring new places, eating ice cream and watching *The Office* on repeat. One would say I'm talented and have an eye for design. I'll just take their word for it.

On a deeper level, I am in a fragile and confusing period of my life right now where I am asking myself, "Who am I? What do I really want in this life?" and I'm a little embarrassed by it all as well because I'm 38 and cannot answer this properly. Shouldn't I have my act together by now? Isn't there some story to tell? How can I *not* know who I am? I'm going through an identity crisis, not only about who am I as a person but who I am as a quilter and artist, blindsided by my spouse's faith crisis (followed by my own), leaving me to question everything.

What is your personal relationship or history with quilts? What draws you to them? What led you to the world of quilts?

I'm the first person in my family to make quilts, so my history with them is still very new. I was introduced to modern quilt making through Danny Heyen back in 2012, and at that time I was seeking blog content and decided to make a quilt for my son. Ever since then, the quilting community has graciously invited me into their fun world of design and art.

I am really driven by design—interior, graphic, architecture and surface, to name a few. I love Amish quilts, and quilts made by the women of Gee's Bend

"I know when to discipline myself and follow the rules, but I just chose to do my own thing as a quilter. If I am conforming to everyone else's ideals and rules, how do I ever find my own voice? If I do not push or challenge boundaries, how can I create new and exciting ideas for myself? Change and comfort cannot coexist."

because good design is found in their works, but I was not introduced to them until after I began quilting. I enjoy the textures derived from weavings like rugs or textiles, and I find that design and texture become one in quilt making, which is satisfying to me. These things, the combination of design and texture, draw me to quilt making. The ability to make designs from my head come to life in 3D form is really fascinating—like, "I really made that??"

How would you describe your style or aesthetic?

I have two different styles of quilting, since I enjoy both very much. One style is improvisational piecing, with potentially busier blocks, lines that may not be as straight and seams that do not match up, and the overall design feels more organic and intuitive. My other style is more geometric in nature, sometimes not as busy, with lines that are straight and seams that match, and the overall design looks more structured and thought out. Black is my signature colour, so I try to incorporate that into my work as much as I can.

More recently, I've been drawn to the nuances found in clothing or the subtle variations from hand-dyed fabric, and I love how these things can keep the movement and interest going in a quilt.

What are your intentions when making a quilt or starting a creative project? What thought processes do you typically go through?

My intentions in quilt making are to fulfill a need to create. For any given quilt of mine, it usually starts off with a sketch. Most times, I will abandon the sketch and revisit it many months later. During those months I wait for the perfect opportunity to manifest itself. Maybe a new fabric has finally come to market that really speaks to me or maybe a sudden urge to see that design come to life overcomes me. The thought pro-

cesses vary depending on what style of quilt I am making. Is it improvisational? Is it geometric? But one overall thought I have anytime I make a quilt is focused on the design: Is it cohesive? How does the design move around the quilt? Is it balanced? Does the design give me any hesitation?

What mindset or attitude do you think is best for quilting? How does quilting affect your mental and physical health?

Learning to let unplanned events go during the quilting process is important. Mistakes happen to most of us. Sometimes these mistakes are good, and sometimes they are frustrating and will derail a project quickly, so learning to let go is a must for me. With this said, making do is equally important and will sometimes yield an even better quilt in the end!

Quilting can be very therapeutic because it is an art form. It's a way to express oneself. One topic that isn't talked about much, and maybe I'm just not aware of it, is that quilting isn't the best for one's physical health. When I first began quilting, I was unaware of the physical toll it had on the body. Not only am I working with lots of fabric and batting, which can be heavy, but I have to place my body and limbs in uncomfortable positions for extended periods of time. I have to take extended breaks to avoid injuries. I made 18 quilts in six months during the making of my quilt book, and I suffered an overuse injury in my arm that will resurface to this very day if I am not careful. I need to be conscientious about chair height, posture and the way I position my body during basting, and I need to let my hands or arms rest a lot if I choose to hand quilt or machine quilt.

What quilt traditions do you hold dear? What quilting conventions do you ignore or challenge?

Two traditions I really admire and use in my own work is hand quilting and repurposing clothing. There's something magical that happens when both are used, together or separately. I like to think I challenge the idea that every quilt must be made the same way using the same rules—quarter-inch seams, pressing to the dark side, press and not iron, wash the fabric first, etc. While I completely understand that these rules have their place and purpose in quilt making, I do not believe that one has to always follow them. This does not mean I wish to construct poorly made quilts. What it does mean is that I allow myself to design and create in a way that suits me, and I give myself the grace needed to express myself in a way that speaks to me because that is what artists do.

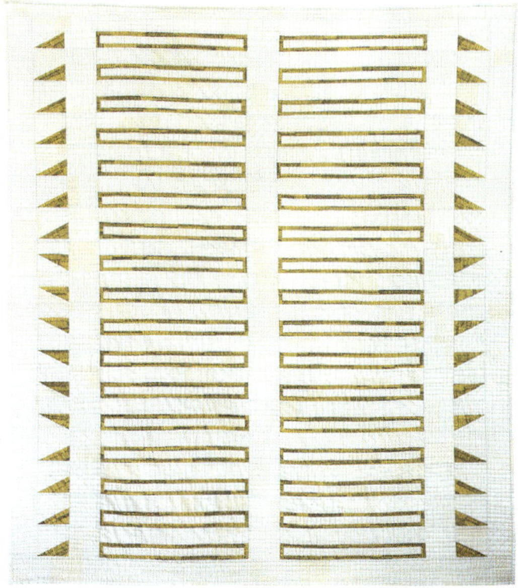

In your opinion or experience, how does the act of quilting bridge the past, present and future?

I hope my small contributions to quilting will one day manifest in my children. The skills I have learned from sewing and quilting would be considered a trade, and not many people are going to schools these days to learn a trade. I do not know many people who can sew. It's a skill that is no longer taught in grade schools. It's easier for some people to buy new instead of mending, or they have misconceptions about the actual costs of supplies and labour, and I totally get it.

"I enjoy using my iPad Pro to paint and draw. I use Photoshop and Illustrator to create designs, paint using watercolours, play around with mark-making and block print to explore new ideas."

Quilting (and sewing), in general, is a trade that is overshadowed by fast-consumerism big-box companies that crank out large quantities at minimal costs and lower quality. As a quilter, I cannot compete with this, but I hope that the more quilters we have in the future, the more people we can teach and educate about handmade, the more we can preserve the skill of sewing, and appreciate and value the time and talent it takes to do it.

What motivates and inspires you?

Design, design and design. I keep sketch journals and photos of anything I find inspiring. I love to refer back to these things because when I look at them, especially if months or years have passed, I get that warm feeling inside me that ignites a creative fire within me. It feels like I can conquer the world and am ready to make something. That feeling is a great motivator for me. If a design I created long ago gets me excited when I see it again after a long time, I know it's a design I want to keep and most likely make.

I am definitely inspired by the world around me, and now that we are more connected than ever before, inspiration is literally at my fingertips. ✻

nancypurvis.com
@nancypurvisstudio

WORKSPACE

My sewing space has changed over the years to accommodate my family's needs. I usually move between our spare bedroom and the kitchen and dining area. I long for a studio space where I can spread out my work and create a wall portfolio of experimentations and in-progress quilting tidbits; a space where community thrives and like-minded artists gather. But for now, I work wherever I can. I sew and iron on my kitchen table and cut fabrics on the kitchen island, or I will sew on the office desk next to my computer. My design wall is a large piece of batting, and it travels from one wall in the home to another, depending on where I am. Basting is done on my living room floor. Because I share my small home with three other people, I have reduced my quilting supplies over the years, which includes my fabric stash, to make room for my family's belongings and hobbies. I purchase supplies only when needed. I guess you could say my studio space is minimal. You may not even know someone sews in my home if you were to walk through it while my machine is put away. It is bittersweet for me. I enjoy there not being clutter, yet I long to be the artist stereotype. I'm following the wise words of Tim Gunn and making it work!

ace&jig Community Quilt Project

by **Cary Vaughan and Jenna Wilson**

"In keeping with our commitment to being a no-waste company, we sent leftover scraps of our fabrics to hundreds of people and each created their own unique quilt square."

With our company, ace&jig, we create clothing from our own custom yarn-dyed and woven textile designs, brought to life by talented weaving partners in India. Our textiles are the beating heart of our collections and we save every last scrap from the cutting room floor as part of our commitment to creating zero waste.

We wanted a way to use these leftover scraps to engage our community and beyond, and it was important to us to create a way for people to be a part of our textile story without having to purchase our clothing. Thus, our Community Quilt Project was born!

We invited anyone who wanted to create a quilt square from our fabric scraps to sign up on our website. For every five sign-ups, we agreed to donate one night-night bag to Project Night Night, a nonprofit organization that gives comforting night bags to children experiencing homelessness. Our goal was to get enough submissions to donate 100 bags. We surpassed this goal in under 24 hours!

Over the next few weeks, we sent 750 bundles of our textile scraps to all who signed up, and hosted events in Portland, Oregon, and New York City where customers could piece together a quilt square in person.

In the end, over 450 one-of-a-kind quilt squares were sent back, and more than 50% of the squares received were made by people who had never purchased our clothing before!

With the help of our friend Adriana Moreno of Moonshadow Goods, we compiled these squares into a series of jumbo quilts, highlighting our amazing community and the many custom woven textiles we've created over the last 10 years. Thirteen quilts were displayed in an exhibit at Brookfield Place in New York City. A few of our volunteers even came, and we helped them locate their squares.

Of all of our no-waste projects over the years, our Community Quilt Project has been our largest and most rewarding, and we are so thankful to all who helped us create and celebrate our largest collaboration yet. ❄

aceandjig.com
@aceandjig

NATALIE EBAUGH

I don't know exactly where my love of textiles comes from. I remember always having an innate and visceral relationship to textiles, especially clothing, when I was very little. Dress-up was my favourite game because I loved that you could create new worlds and a new life for yourself depending on the clothing you chose. Clothing holds our histories and at the same time can weave new stories for us. It's costume, it's how we show ourselves to the world and it's how we tell our own story.

I followed my love of textile and clothing to art school, where I studied fibre arts with a focus in experimental fashion. In the seven or so years since college, I've been creating quilted clothing.

What is your personal relationship or history with quilts? What draws you to them? What led you to the world of quilts?

My interest in quilting started when I found the book *Quilts to Wear* by Virginia Avery. Part instructional and part catalogue, the book highlights a range of styles of quilted clothing and techniques for making them. I was so inspired by this book that I started experimenting first with incorporating quilted panels into jackets.

I love the utilitarian nature of quilts and the fact that people put so much thought and love and energy into these objects that are made to keep us warm. I started making quilted clothing because I love the idea of wearing an object that's filled with so much history and energy.

"I love mixing colours and prints to create unexpected combinations, creating a style that is bold and playful. The garments I create are usually very simple and utilitarian in form to allow for the textiles to shine."

PHOTOS BY REBEKAH FINK

What are your intentions when making a quilt or starting a creative project? What thought processes do you typically go through?

I keep the process intuitive and spontaneous. Sometimes I start out with an idea of the kind of blocks or techniques I want to use and then it evolves from there. I'm not great at sketching my ideas and I often feel like I need to just make the thing instead of thinking and planning too much. Maybe it begins with one colour or textile, or a combination of either, and then the process flows. I want anyone who comes into contact with my work to feel alive and inspired by something unexpected.

What mindset or attitude do you think is best for quilting?

Let go of perfection. Whatever part of the quilting process you are in—cutting, piecing, quilting, binding—be kind to yourself. You are human and you are creating something; you may make mistakes, but that's how we learn. It doesn't matter if your corners don't match up, or your seams are wonky, or even if it falls apart—

embrace it! No one will ever notice your mistakes as much as you do. Let go and enjoy the process.

Both piecing and quilting on the longarm are improvisational processes for me. It's a time when I can tune out the world, almost like a meditative practice.

Have you ever had a quilting or creative failure? What happened? What did you learn from it, if anything?

I have a whole box of partially finished quilt tops that I grew sick of during the creative process. I'm not sure I would necessarily call these failures. Sometimes you spend too much time with a piece and need to give it a timeout so that you can return to it with new appreciation. I've learned that it's helpful to give myself some breathing room with projects because it helps me from overthinking the project. Every piece is reflective of the time and space in which it was made, and I enjoy revisiting them, even if they were never finished.

How does the act of quilting bridge the past, present and future?

Quilting has so many traditional techniques that I and many others in the community use in our work, and many new techniques that allow us to do things with our quilts that would have been much more difficult, if not impossible, in the past. Any one of my own pieces may have used old techniques, new techniques or more often a combination of both. I think the accessibility of modern techniques helps expose more people to quilting in general while encouraging the traditional methods to live on as people explore the craft. Each generation of quilts will tell their own story with the techniques used to make them, pulling from past and present, and paving the way for future quilters.

When and how did you become a professional?

I would say that I became a professional when I landed my first big commission job. In December 2017, I was contacted by Jenna Wilson, one of the founders of the clothing brand ace&jig, inquiring about a collaboration. ace&jig is a clothing company with an amazing no-waste mission. Since their textiles are custom made in India, the brand founders collaborate with textiles artists to put their fabric scraps to use. I have created a total of 25 quilted coats for the brand using only their fabric scraps, and this past April, 15 of the coats were featured in a sustainable fashion pop-up event hosted by Nordstrom.

This collaboration has been huge for me. I've learned and grown so much professionally, creatively and personally. Prior to this experience, I had the desire to sell my quilted pieces, but I didn't have the confidence. Sometimes a little outside validation, whether from a commission, sale or just a single person who admires your work, can be a big motivator to keep creating.

What breadth of activity and responsibilities do you have as a professional quilter?

At the moment I teach an intro to longarm quilting class, which I've done for about three years in various stores and studios that rent longarm machines to sewists. This next year I plan to release a pattern for one of my quilted jackets. I'm excited to share it and see what other sewists make with it!

Are you able to support yourself in the quilt industry or do you have other endeavours as well?

Quilting has always been a side hustle for me. For the past seven years, I've worked in sewing stores and worn a number of hats within those positions, including managing, buying, educating and marketing.

"I find inspiration in many different traditional styles of quilting, but I'm not a purist by any means. In art school, we were taught that as artists your job is to learn the techniques and rules of your craft and then challenge and break those rules."

WORKSPACE

I share a home sewing studio with my sister in the master bedroom of the house. We have a cutting table, a table for our sewing machines and a table for our sergers, and a couple of shelving units filled with fabric, plus other fabric scattered around here and there. We work in the studio daily, before or after work, on various projects. I love that we can spend time together, working side by side, and the creative energy that happens when we're both in there. We dance around each other as we work and clean up after each other. I love that I can wake up early to work or stay up late, and my bedroom is just a few feet away. We are very lucky to have the space we have. I'm very grateful for it.

My full-time jobs have allowed me the financial stability and support to make my quilting and sewing dreams come true. Having a full-time job means that my studio time is limited, but it also takes the financial pressure off of my creative practice, allowing me to just make things without worrying about whether or not I need to sell them. The sewing community is amazing to work in and I feel lucky to spend much of my time with people who share my passion.

What motivates and inspires you?

Learning and gaining new experiences are my main motivators. I've always had a need or drive to create and I love the process of making and learning, especially within sewing. I'm a self-taught quilter, so I always appreciate learning new techniques and tips to improve my craft.

Do any particular ideas, objects or activities—outside of and unrelated to quilting—inform and inspire your quilting practice?

I am inspired by so many things! Paintings, illustration, fashion, movies, cartoons and more. I can't even name them all! I use Pinterest to gather inspiring images. It's really helpful to have one place to organize ideas and images to return to later. I don't use a sketchbook, so Pinterest is that for me. ✻

natalie-ebaugh.com
@natalie_ebaugh

PATRICIA BELYEA

I made my first quilt when I was 53, for a gal in my office who was having a baby girl. I borrowed a sewing machine, got old clothes at Goodwill, bought what I thought was a good pair of scissors and attended a church quilt group meeting. The founder of the quilt group, Maurine Noble, advised me to make a Split Rail pattern for my first quilt. When I showed Maurine my finished quilt, her generous praise encouraged me to make a second quilt. And then another and another!

Within five years of making my first quilt, I quit the corporate design world and became a full-time quilter. By that time, I had begun importing vintage textiles from Japan that I used in my own projects, as well as sold to others. And I wrote a book, *East-Meets-West Quilts*, about making improv quilts with Japanese fabrics.

As a quilter full of curiosity, I've sought new ways to sew fabrics together. Through trial and error, I developed my own technique for piecing quilt tops filled with curves. Most recently I've begun a series of quilts where I create a patchwork grid and then insert curved design elements.

"Although I was a late starter, I believe that everything in my life led me to be a quilter. Quilting is my calling. I love the graphic quality of quilts, the act of making and the final, tangible product."

What is your personal relationship or history with quilts? What draws you to them? What led you to the world of quilts?

My Belyea ancestors had an inn on a byway in one of Canada's eastern provinces. The upstairs rooms were filled with brass beds topped with simple two-colour quilts. For added warmth, there were extra layers of utility blankets—hand-stitched whole cloth quilts made of white cotton.

In a more recent generation, my Grandmother Belyea described attending weekly quilting bees to

PHOTOS BY LINDSEY MILLER, ROSANNE OLSON AND PATRICIA BELYEA

“I'm not interested in making a quilt that someone else has made. Instead, I challenge myself to produce something that has never been seen before.”

stitch the quilts of her fellow church members. My own mother, in her 70s, became a wildly ingenious quilter—making small projects with vivid colours and crazy machine piecing. These concoctions, with bobbin nests on the undersides and sloppy bindings all around, are highly prized today by her six offspring.

I did not start quilting to follow any family traditions. All the same, once I started quilting, I gained a shared passion with my mother. Whenever I visited, I brought my mom exciting fabrics or really nice quilting tools. Once we tried to make a quilt top together but my mom, at that time in her 80s, said that I exhausted her with my counterintuitive ways of piecing. Then Mom asked for me to stop and go out for lunch with her. I finished that quilt on my own.

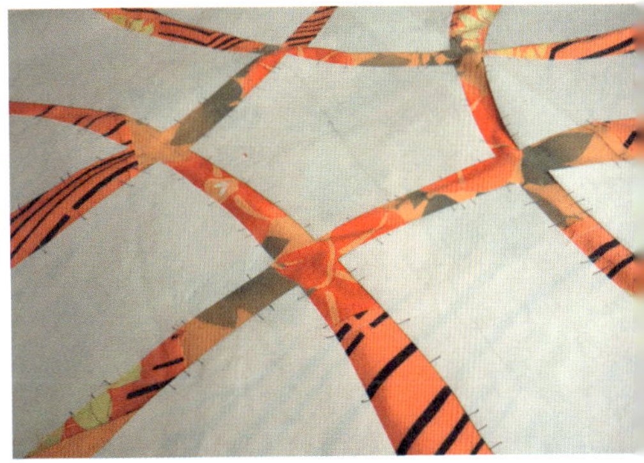

How would you describe your style or aesthetic?

My quilting style does not land squarely in any typical quilt camp—traditional quilting, modern quilting or art quilting. My aesthetic is simple and my fabrics are global. I like to say that my quilts are creative. And someone was kind enough to say to me, "your quilts are full of integrity."

I have a background as a graphic designer so I'm interested in developing relationships with colour and form within my quilt compositions. All the same, I like to push past my own comfort zones to combine fabrics in ways that don't conform with my long-held beliefs of what should go together.

Typically my quilt tops are filled with curved piecing and my fabrics are remarkable Japanese cottons. Together they combine to create something out of the ordinary.

What are your intentions or thought processes when making a quilt or starting a creative project?

I keep a journal in my purse that's filled with little quilt sketches. I draw little boxes on the page and then fill in each box with line work. When I am looking for design inspiration, these are useful to look through. My sketching can happen in cars or airplanes, or when I am in a waiting mode. I think that if I just look around, there's something that can spark a sketch—a shape, a line, a word. I will take just one idea and keep drawing variations until I fill up all the boxes on the page. This helps me leapfrog my original idea and land somewhere completely different than where I started.

What mindset or attitude do you think is best for quilting? How does quilting affect your mental and physical health?

It's a joy to get totally involved in any aspect of quilt making and I always have a solid sense of accomplishment with the last stitch. My favourite activity is to work in my studio. When I have lots of energy, I work on ambitious design challenges. At the end of the day, when my stamina is ebbing, I do repetitive work or quiet hand stitching. My bliss is to work on quilting projects every day. It brings me true happiness and a sense of balance.

What quilt traditions do you hold dear? What quilting conventions do you ignore or challenge?

Decades ago quilts were made with fabrics that the makers had in their lives—castaway clothes, worn-out linens and anything else they could get their hands on. In that tradition, I'm a treasure hunter. The act of discovery adds adventure to my work. Early on I acquired my fabrics from free boxes and thrift stores, and through the generosity of other quilters downsizing their stashes. Now I scour Japan for vintage yukata cottons that I import for myself and others.

In your opinion or experience, how does the act of quilting bridge the past, present and future?

Not only does quilting reach across the span of time, but quilting can also be found all around the globe. I own a late Meiji-era sleeping kimono from Japan. It's a huge kimono, filled with wads of cotton and stitched together by hand. Inside and out are little patches sewn on boro-style to keep the kimono from losing its padding, as it was used for generations.

For me, quilting evokes warmth and comfort. The appeal of these simple human values is universal over time and place.

Would you consider yourself as a professional within the quilting industry? When and how did you become a professional?

My passion for quilting and playing with Japanese cottons transformed into an enterprise when I returned from a trip to Tokyo in January 2009. The next day I filed with the IRS, Washington state and the City of Seattle to receive the appropriate paperwork and licenses to run a quilting business.

At first, I sold vintage Japanese textiles at little weekend events. In January 2013, I quit my corporate job and became a full-time quilter. I've since expanded my business activities to include week-long workshops and retreats, as well as special events. I've also begun offering textile tours to Japan that are tailored for quilters.

Okan Arts supports me and my daughter and co-owner, Victoria Stone. Besides quilt making, I keep busy travelling and teaching while Victoria runs the shop. ✻

WORKSPACE

I have two homes—a historical wooden house in Seattle and a pine log cabin in the Okanogan Highlands. In both places, I have a quilting studio. Neither are big and both sit right in the centre of the action with no doors to close out my family.

I like to have my studio at home, as I just might get started on a project in my pajamas in the morning or work late into the night after dinner.

I don't need much to get to work—a dependable sewing machine, a high-powered iron and wide ironing board, and a big design wall. Plus impeccable scissors and good thread. I have parallel gear in both spaces so one studio does not feel inferior to the other.

Tidy as a pin between projects, either studio looks like a creative tornado hit it when I'm engrossed in my work. Although the studio gets dishevelled, the piles are in constant motion as the quilt design begins to get resolved. As I like to say, I can't get creative if I can't get messy.

okanarts.com
@okanarts

Some Of It Remains

by **Heather Jones**

"Through trial and error, I began to use fabric in a painterly manner. While there is no paint in these works, I refer to them as paintings. Conceptually, my work carries on the tradition of women as makers, pushes the boundary between fine art and craft, and questions the definition of painting."

Some Of It Remains was one of the first pieces that I made after a trip to Marrakech in February 2019. I had been working mostly in black-and-white for the past couple of years, but wanted to make a change, and I felt a pull to work with more colours. I found Morocco incredibly inspiring, and I was excited to get to work in the studio and see what its effect would be.

I began the piece by working from scraps from leftover projects and sewing them together, creating quasi–quilt blocks, although they were not square or uniform at all. Once these segments got to a certain size, I would put each one on my design wall and start on another. I played with the composition, rotating a component or two, and sometimes adding additional fabric as I joined all of the parts. Once the composition was sewn together, I stretched it around a wooden support, stapling it on the back to hold everything in place. The fabric is pulled quite taut, so seams start to shift and stretch, which adds more movement and organic lines to the finished piece. This element of chance that plays a role in the final composition is one of my favourite parts of the technique.

This piece belongs to a body of work that I started right around the time that my book *Quilt Local: Finding Inspiration in the Everyday* (Abrams, 2015) was released. I wanted to paint again, which I hadn't done regularly in about a decade, but I wanted to make paintings like my quilts, with areas of colour and geometric shapes, rather than the representational art that I had made in the past. ❋

heatherjonesstudio.com
@heatherjonesstudio

RIANE MENARDI MORRISON

I am a modern quilter, designer and writer making minimal quilts for the modern home. I found my way to quilting nearly 10 years ago and started working in the industry in 2015. I was the communications manager for the Modern Quilt Guild for four years, and then moved to Quiltfolk in 2019 to serve as their brand director. I've worn many hats during my time in the quilt industry, but I mostly create creative content for quilters—whether it be through pattern development, directing photoshoots, or writing articles and collaborating with others. In my own quilting, I tend to gravitate towards simple shapes, clean lines and hand-finished elements like hand quilting and hand piecing.

PHOTOGRAPHY BY AUSTIN DAY, STYLING BY LAUREN DAY

What is your personal relationship or history with quilts? What draws you to them? What led you to the world of quilts?

I fell into the world of quilts by accident—or maybe quilts found me. When I was fresh out of college, I asked my grandmother to teach me how to sew. I wanted to learn how to make my own clothes, but she bought me a quilt pattern instead and set me loose with her scraps. We made my first quilt together, and I learned the art of piecing and hand quilting. I didn't know at the time how important that skill would be and how it would change my life. It's humbling to step into that ritual of learning to quilt from a family member, and now that I work in the industry, each quilt I make reminds me of that lineage and the tradition. I fell so hard for quilting that I never did learn how to sew garments.

"I love that a handmade quilt can never be replicated, so each quilt is as unique to me as a fingerprint."

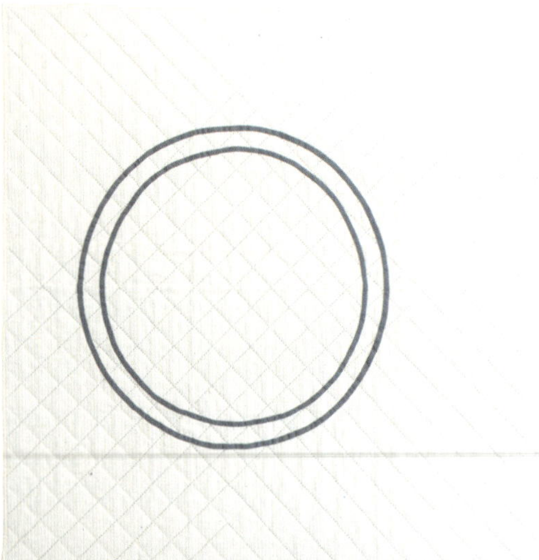

How would you describe your style?

My style is handcrafted and minimalist. I use simple colour palettes and solid fabrics to create thoughtful design elements and lots of negative space. I also finish all my quilts by hand using high-contrast hand quilting that complements the piecing and stands alone as its own design element. Instead of the quilting being an afterthought, I design the quilt as a whole with the quilting motif already in mind before I even start sewing. I also use the same materials in every quilt—a linen/cotton blend fabric, thick cotton thread and wool batting. I love the materials and want to let them shine on their own, and restraining the materials in this way helps me focus on creating interest in the piecing and quilting designs.

What are your intentions when making a quilt or starting a creative project? What thought processes do you typically go through?

I love making quilts because they allow us to own the entire process—from designing a quilt on the computer to piecing each seam and quilting each stitch. I love the ownership of the process, and I think my intention when quilting is to create something truly meaningful by infusing meaning into the design, colours, materials and construction methods. I design quilts in collections, and often they represent a larger theme in my life at the time. The Inheritance quilts from my book all represent my idea of home and were designed and made shortly after I got married. I'm currently working on a Crossroads series that represents moving from Des Moines to Denver, as well as the season of work and transition that has been the major theme in my life during this time.

What mindset or attitude do you think is best for quilting? How does quilting affect your mental and physical health?

I like that each part of the process requires different creative energy. I love the creative play that happens during the design process. For piecing, I like high-energy music and several hours to cut, sew and press while dancing around my studio. Basting and marking lines is my least favourite part of the process, but it's the most important. Good basting and marking leads to straight stitches and a flat finished quilt, so my mindset during this phase is very focused. Quilting and hand binding is my favourite part of the process, and a great way to relax—I watch movies or TV shows, and I love to keep my hands busy.

Quilting feeds my soul through all of these different creative phases, and each step has its own mental benefits for me. Physically, it's really important to counter the hours of sitting with something that restores my body. For me, a hot yoga practice is the perfect complement to quilting, and I'm most happy when my body, mind and creativity are aligned.

Have you ever had a quilting or creative failure? What happened? What did you learn from it, if anything?

So many! I tend to run before I walk, and overconfidence is often my downfall. I've made more math and cutting mistakes than I care to admit, and I've wasted a lot of time, money and fabric. My early patterns all had wrong math, and one of the biggest mistakes I made was while teaching a Block of the Month class

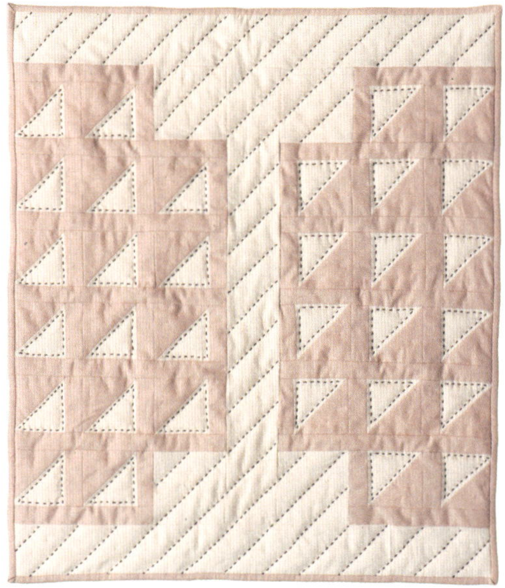

at my local quilt shop. I got the backing yardage wrong in the pattern and my students weren't able to finish their quilts properly during one of our sessions. I felt horrible, and I learned to be more thoughtful with my process, especially when it will affect others. I also learned that quilt math is not my forte, and I should always hire a technical editor.

What quilt traditions do you hold dear? What quilting conventions do you ignore or challenge?

I really value the tradition of hand quilting, and lately hand piecing. Often, life can be about the churn—fast finishes, posting the perfect Instagram photo every day, waiting for the next new thing. I like the slowness of handwork, and all the soft, crinkly handmade quilts in my home are my favourites.

One quilting convention that I tend to reject is the use of blocks. I like to create modern designs by approaching a quilt as a whole rather than by piecing blocks. My quilts are made using traditional methods but with more modern designs.

In your opinion or experience, how does the act of quilting bridge the past, present and future?

Oh, I love this question. I called my book *Inheritance* because I truly feel like quilting is a skill that is passed down through generations, just like a family heirloom or tradition. Whether you learn to quilt from a grandmother or from a YouTube video, anyone who takes up quilting is part of that history and lineage, and we're making quilts today in the same way that people have been making them for centuries. The popular designs and patterns may have changed over the years, but a love for quilting ties us to past generations and allows us to share this inheritance with our families and friends, and continue the cycle. I also love how every quilt is different, and there is no one type of quilter—anyone, regardless of class, race, gender, etc., can make a quilt and step into that ritual. You don't need a fancy machine or special tools; you just need fabric, batting, needle, thread and a will to start.

When and how did you become a professional?

I studied journalism and communications in college, then transitioned to marketing after being unable to land a journalism job after the recession. I built a specialty for myself in creating content for creative professionals within the handmade and DIY space. I also did quilting as a side hustle, and I produced quilts and wrote freelance articles for *Fresh Quilts* magazine, thanks to my friend and mentor, Deb Gore Ohrn, who hired me to work on the magazine. In 2015, I was hired as the communications manager for the Modern Quilt Guild, and in 2019, I joined team Quiltfolk as their brand director. I feel lucky every day that I get to be surrounded by quilting in my day job, and I love working in a hobby industry. I also continue to build my own brand on the side, and I sell books and patterns, and teach around the country.

What breadth of activity and responsibilities do you have as a professional quilter?

These days it's mostly creative direction and brand development. For Quiltfolk, I help design and curate products, plan and direct product photoshoots, and help with creative marketing and brand direction. For the Modern Quilt Guild, I helped with marketing and programming, and I worked with contributors on webinars, patterns and resources. I've also managed social media and email marketing, and networked and collaborated on behalf of organizations and brands. I have also cowritten a few books, including *Modern Quilts: Designs of the New Century* and *Smithsonian for Makers*, due out in 2020.

In my own work, I've self-published my own book, *Inheritance: Minimal Quilts for the Modern Home*. I have a line of print and digital patterns, and I teach modern quilting design and techniques.

Are you able to support yourself in the quilt industry or do you have other endeavours as well?

Yes, I support myself almost entirely in the quilt industry, mostly through my day job. However, I do earn a small percentage of my income through my personal quilting endeavours like book sales, pattern sales and teaching.

What motivates and inspires you?

Social media is a double-edged sword, but I find a lot of motivation in seeing what others are creating, in quilting and other crafts. I heard once that your "before" is someone else's "after," and I think that's true. Everyone had to start somewhere. Recognizing that progression has motivated me to take the next step. I don't always have the time, energy or resources to do everything I want, but I can take one step (maybe designing a collection that I love), and lay the groundwork for

taking the next step. I like to think of it as setting myself up for success, and I often thank "past Riane" for the work she's done, even if she didn't know where it would lead. So far it's worked out, and I've learned that if I show up each day, do the work and trust myself and my process, good things tend to happen.

Do any particular ideas, objects or activities—outside of and unrelated to quilting—inform and inspire your quilting practice?

I'm very inspired by home and interior design and trends in furniture, illustration and photography. I fell in love with design during an internship at *ReadyMade* magazine almost 10 years ago, and since then I've developed my own tastes and style. For the Inheritance quilts, I had just planned a wedding, and the colours and imagery from the wedding industry were very fresh in my mind. Today, I'm being inspired by the colours and shapes trending in the home and design worlds—specifically warm tones, minimal aesthetics and pops of whimsy. ✻

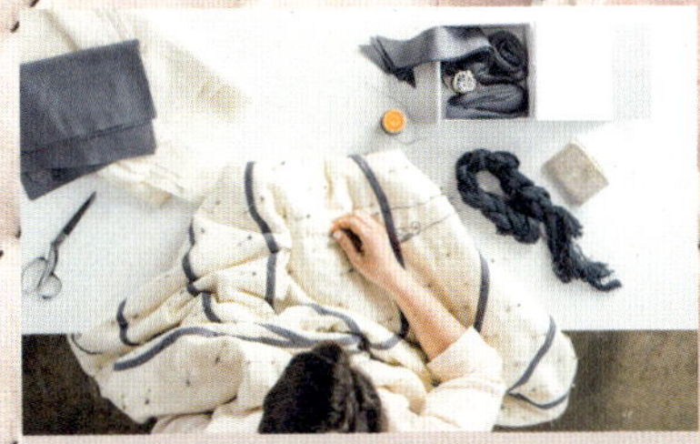

WORKSPACE

My husband and I recently moved from a three-storey house into a small apartment when we relocated to Denver. I used to have an attic studio with a big table and lots of built-in storage, but now, many of my tools and supplies are in storage, and I don't have a dedicated space to quilt in. I pared down my stash to a small cabinet that holds my most-loved supplies (mostly linen, wool batting and hand-quilting thread). My small space is actually a big reason I've incorporated more hand piecing into my work, and at least for this season, I like keeping a minimalist studio and using the lack of space and storage almost as a creative constraint. My quilts now are more thoughtful and more simplistic (also smaller), but they are made with techniques that are new to me like hand piecing that help infuse more meaning into my work.

riane-elise.com
@riane.elise

SCOTT HANSEN

I grew up in the country playing in the woods when the weather was good or making stuff inside when it wasn't. I never liked games or sports when I was a kid, and we didn't have the electronic gadgetry kids have today. I always wanted to be making something. My mom kept us busy with crafty things. In the early years, that always involved paper, crayons, markers, scissors, glue, etc. When I was 12, I got a Tandy leather kit. From about 15 to 18, I painted plaster figures, including an enormous nativity set.

Mom kept herself busy sewing for our family, but she never created quilts. She showed me how to crochet and embroider, but I wasn't able to stay interested in it for long enough back then. I did learn to sew. My first sewing project was a stuffed raccoon when I was about 10 and my first quilt was when I was about 14. It was a crazy quilt and my mom helped me, but neither of us knew what we were doing. We just winged it.

I will have been married for 30 years in October this year. It's hard to believe that much time has gone by. Over those three decades, and three kids, a smattering of cats, chickens, ducks and one dog, my wife and I together discovered that we had the hearts and souls of artists. My media is primarily in quilting; my wife's is more mixed-media.

What is your personal relationship or history with quilts? What draws you to them? What led you to the world of quilts?

Growing up, my dad liked all things new but my mom was thrifty. She kept and reused as much of the old as possible. I always liked the old stuff better. We had two quilts that I remember seeing growing up, but they weren't on my parent's "good stuff" list.

"I have more ideas than I have time to create. If I ever hit a creative slump, I can always go back to a sketch, or finish up one of my many works in progress."

The US Bicentennial happened in the middle of my childhood, so all things colonial was the trend in my two major influencers: school and TV. I was quite taken with thinking that historical life was the best thing ever. The history associated with antiques intrigued me a great deal, including that of quilts.

Ten years later, I married Linda, who collected antiques and vintage fashion. She knew a great deal more about history than I did, as her parents instilled an appreciation of it in her. So as we were setting up house, we picked up some vintage quilts. We happened to check out a quilt show just for fun; I had never seen so many at one time. I was inspired to make more of my own quilts. So I bought a book and a sewing machine and started teaching myself about standard construction methods. I didn't realize the importance of accurate quarter-inch seams and had not heard of a rotary cutter. I just started making. Over time, I met other quilters, joined guilds and discovered that rotary cutter and more accurate piecing practices. But the whole time I was also discovering so many different approaches and attitudes about quilt design and construction.

How would you describe your style or aesthetic?

My style has both changed and stayed the same over the last 25 years of my quilting journey. When I first started quilting constantly, I was enamoured with country colours and rustic style. Linda always joked that my favourite colour was "brown plaid" and that I could not make a quilt without crows or pumpkins. My choices shifted in a more modern direction with the discovery of Kaffe Fassett and Amy Butler fabrics about 15 years ago. My palette has come full circle, though, as I have been returning to some of those country colours and combining them with the bright, clear, crisp modern colours I am now known for.

I live near urban centres and frequent them often, but always feel a bit more at home in rural areas. Both of these worlds greatly influence my designs and vision. My favourite quilts mix everything up: colour, value, scale and prints from all sorts of designers. I have dubbed my style "urban folk." Lots of straight lines evoke the urban aspect (I avoid actual curves normally) but the wonky and unusual formats add the folk quality.

What are your intentions when making a quilt or starting a creative project? What thought processes do you typically go through?

When I start a quilt, it usually has been brewing in my head for a while. I am constantly writing and drawing ideas. I have thousands of scraps of paper with sketches or notes describing ideas! These sketches go to graph paper or to my computer in Illustrator. I usually have an idea of the colour scheme, but rarely have the fabric picked out ahead of time. I like to let the fabric speak to me before I decide on its final resting spot in the quilt.

Probably the most important factor I try to consider even above colour choices is the value placement of the fabric in the quilt layout. I love contrasts of all sorts. Mixing stripes with florals. Large florals with teensy dots. Novelty prints with solids. I rarely plan the binding at the same time as the quilt—I do default to striped bindings when the right fabric surfaces.

I also consider the temperature of the colours, often making sure to separate or combine colours based on the look I am going for. Hot colours with cool colours in a myriad of combinations.

I rarely concern myself with the final outcome. I am constantly amazed by how much more I like the quilt in real life than in my sketches. Sometimes when the design is particularly strong, I think, "Wow, that came out pretty darn good!"

"For me, it is totally relaxing just playing with fabric, needles and fibre in a myriad of ways.

As I get older I am being drawn to the concept of creating more art for the sake of art and for making a statement."

What mindset or attitude do you think is best for quilting? How does quilting affect your mental and physical health?

Perfection is a nice goal but not necessary by any means. In fact, I rather embrace the imperfections of my work now and enjoy the process of mixing fabric and fibres in a unique and intriguing way.

I am drawn to handwork. Our world seems to be getting more and more separated at the same time as technology is drawing us together. I like the escape from all of the electronic impulses vying for our attention. When I am in the studio, I might have music on, but never news or TV shows. I am even known to have the windows open in the early morning so I can hear the birds of the forest and the sounds of our neighbourhood waking up. I just feel so complete when I am sewing. This is who God made me to be.

What quilt traditions do you hold dear? What quilting conventions do you ignore or challenge?

I love using a variety of scraps. I feel such a connection to each piece of fabric I use, and though my scraps are

not from other household sewing projects, as those in many vintage quilts often are, I have this sense of connection to both my past and the heritage of the quilt-making tradition.

I love seeing my paper design come to life in the fabrics. Sometimes it comes out exactly as I had hoped, and other times I am taken completely by surprise. I do not strive for perfection in my work, though; I am quite satisfied with perfect imperfection. I get very excited when cutting into new fabric for the first time. I love the stacks of beautiful designs waiting to be included in one of my creations.

I don't do most of my own quilting; I usually hire it out, and my ultimate favourite thing about the return of the now quilted quilt is the binding of it. I love the hand stitching part of binding the most. I feel a sense of completion and success and gratitude and joy in that process. It relaxes me! If the quilt is a gift, I often use that time to pray for blessings for the recipient.

In your opinion or experience, how does the act of quilting bridge the past, present and future?

There is such a history of quiltmaking and so many quilters over centuries of human interactions with needle and cloth. I don't know if I actually consider that in everyday life, but it is so true.

There have been so many styles of quilting, and in my lifetime I am sure to only scratch the surface of the different concepts and techniques.

Above all, I believe we are all created beings from the one Creator, and as such, each of us has been blessed with a creative aptitude of sorts. Not all of us discover this creativity, but I am happy to be amongst the great group of quilters I find myself in. And in spite of its many perils and problems, I am grateful for the Internet, and along with that the modern modes of communication and travel that have brought me into contact with so many different quilters from far away places and other philosophies. Quilters of the past did not have the instantaneous input from their quilting friends as we do today. I am so pleased with the wide circle of friends in my life that my quilting obsession has currently gifted me with.

When and how did you become a professional?

My professional life in the quilting industry began over such a long course of time that I didn't even know it was happening at the time. But I think what really started it was the very first *Quilt Sampler* magazine back in 1994. I had been wanting to run a quilt shop, as I had liked many elements of being in a retail job, and here was a magazine that featured the top 10 shops in North America. Through that first issue, I met Mary Etherington and Connie Tesene from the shop Country Threads. Within a few months after meeting them (via letters and phone, mind you, this was *way* before our many current communication conveniences), they invited me to help them at Quilt Market, which happened to be a few hours away in Portland, Oregon. Talk about a *giant* quilt show! I was bitten bad by both the quilting bug and a dream to somehow become part of that industry.

Over time, I started submitting quilts to magazines and then volunteering to help designers and fabric companies at Quilt Market. I started a blog, and somehow my quilt design business, now called Blue Nickel Studios, was birthed.

What breadth of activity and responsibilities do you have as a professional quilter?

To date, I have designed two lines of modern batiks for Banyan Batiks. I have PDF patterns for sale in my online shop and paper patterns in local quilt shops. I am working on at least five new patterns that I am behind on writing up because that is my second least favourite part of quilting as a business (my least favourite part is the paperwork!).

As my limited time off from my day job allows, I get out a few times a year to teach classes based on my patterns and trunk shows. My favourite part of the business aspect of my quilting journey is this sharing of my quilts and stories with other quilters. I get energized and inspired by my students and their interpretations of my patterns. Plus, I experience a very deep sense of community in the presence of other quilters, designers, teachers and students.

Are you able to support yourself in the quilt industry or do you have other endeavours as well?

I currently work at Costco resolving IT problems for employees five days a week. This pays our mortgage and takes care of our health insurance. Our subsistence comes from that income. I have not yet worked in the quilt industry for our sole income. Part of our downsizing plan in the near future is to get a better

but smaller home with a minimal or non-existent mortgage, and in doing so, cut back my Costco hours to devote more time to this world. Costco is basically my second act in life. The quilting professional life is the plan for the third act—working my way toward that is the goal. Linda wants me to teach and lecture all over the world, so she can travel with me to far away places as my "handler."

What motivates and inspires you?

Most days, I have so many ideas and so much fabric collected that motivation to hit the studio is not a problem. I simply feel compelled from deep within to create. Usually that inner coaxing settles itself in the quilting realm, although I sometimes like to make rustic bits of furniture as well—mostly shelves, benches, footstools or occasionally garden art. I am not sure what life would be like if I wasn't always creating. I am very fidgety if I don't have something to keep my hands busy. The last few years, I have picked up embroidery as a portable creative diversion. When I was a kid, I wasn't happy with my imperfect stitches; now I revel in them. ✻

bluenickelstudios.com
@bluenickelstudios

WORKSPACE

My wife and I share a studio in the upper bonus room in the house we built. Linda is looking forward to moving her studio into one of the kids' bedrooms because my side tends to invade her side. We are looking to downsize and move to a more remote location (on an island!) in the next few years, so the studio is in a bit of a compression mode. When I say downsize, I only mean the house part, not the studio. I think that will be larger, while our actual living space will be considerably less, now that our kids are on their own. We need more space to create, but we only need a few rooms for the two of us to live in.

I am not a tidy or organized quilter. I like seeing all of the fabric and trims and buttons, etc. This invigorates me, but I also do often lose things in the studio because something else gets put on top of it. This would drive most people batty, including Linda, who is ever so tidy. I revel in it most days, with occasional bouts of cleaning that honestly never last long enough. I know I have books and fabric that I won't see until we move.

Sunday Best

by **Michelle Wilkie**

Sunday Best started off as a project to escape the stress of deadlines, work and just general life activities. There was no real plan. No colour palette. I just wanted to play with my solid scraps (excluding most neutrals) for two hours every Sunday—you know, to give myself some me time.

This time added up, allowing me to explore and reflect on the things that I didn't know I needed. The black-and-white triangles were added as I was thinking of my mum who was suffering from a terminal illness and saddened to think this might be her last Mother's Day. I just did not feel like colour that day. In the end, the black-and-white added a balance to the quilt and a place to rest. I really enjoyed the process and was eager to see what happened each week. After 10 weeks, this was the result. ❋

"I needed a creative reboot and a project that involved little to no planning, no stress—just free playing around."

ideadesigncreatequilt.com/portfolio
@ml_wilkie

SHARON McCONNELL

I am the original Colorful Quilter! It is my mission to encourage every quilter to be their most colourful self. That might mean going all out and sewing a rainbow into every quilt. It also means that each person I reach when I teach workshops or share my quilting designs feels inspired to foster their creativity to the fullest and most free. I love to see quilters try a new skill, colour scheme or fabric style and fall in love with the art of quilt making all over again.

> "The thing that first drew me into quilting is still what I love most about it: pattern. Something about an interesting arrangement of shapes and colours makes my heart happy."

Quilting is such a unique and inspiring pastime. There are so many steps in the process, from choosing a pattern, colours and fabric, to the physical making, and enjoying a finished quilt. I have found each step to be a time for exploring and learning. It's a process that brings me a lot of happiness, positive energy and creative fulfillment.

I grew up in a family of quilters. We had quilts that were made by great-grandmothers. My maternal grandmother always had a frame set up in her living room where she hand quilted for anyone she knew having a baby. My mother sewed my clothes and always had a quilt she was working on.

The first quilt I sewed was with her scraps when I was a child. Quilting became a serious interest to me as a young adult just out of college, living in a new city and knowing exactly one person. It became a way to make friends: classes at

local shops, and quilting in church basements with ladies who could be my grandmothers. It's also a connection to my mother. After I left home, we built our visits around sewing: trips to quilt shows and shops, and holing up just to make quilts together.

How would you describe your style or aesthetic?

I consider myself a traditional quilter with a modern aesthetic. I am also a modern quilter using traditional techniques. I suppose some might say these are contradictory. My quilts aren't "modern" as defined by the community at large, but I am a modern quilter in that I prefer saturated colours and contemporary fabrics and striking patterns. I am a traditional quilter in that I prefer all-over, repeated patterns and blocks rather than asymmetrical designs or leaving negative space. I am right in that happy medium: I'm a modern traditionalist, and at the end of the day I sew because it's enjoyable and I make what I like, not what is necessarily trendy or fits anyone else's definition.

What are your intentions when making a quilt? What thought processes do you typically go through?

The creative process is what makes quilting such a fulfilling art form. The many steps required keep it interesting, and there are several points along the way where I make decisions and may change course.

The first step is matching the chosen design with the perfect fabric. I start with a small-ish selection of fabrics and colours. I am more constrained by what goes together at this stage. As I get sewing, though, I add more variety: different prints in the same colours and more variations on colour. My favourite way to add interest to a quilt is by using a variety of fabrics to represent a single colour. A finished project doesn't always look like the original concept. It's fun to be flexible during the process: rearranging and rotating blocks to explore new layouts, or adding a different block, colour or shape to alternate with what I started with for a more complicated look. Sometimes the designs that evolve the most during the process are the ones I like the best when finished.

"I am always noticing colours. I especially love flowers, plants and textures in the natural world and tend to translate those images to my colour palette. I really enjoy drawing and would love to learn to paint. I think that when you enjoy making and creative activities, all of your interests and hobbies, as well as everyday life, start to come together to influence your style."

"A creative passion should be an exploration: sometimes you know where you are going, other times you are making it up as you go. Nothing too precious, no worries about doing it wrong, no constraints except the ones we want—that's what has kept me loving quilting year after year."

What mindset or attitude do you think is best for quilting? How does quilting affect your mental and physical health?

Quilting is a requirement to keep me sane and happy. It helps me unwind and forget stressors.

I think it's important to be open to trying new ideas, colours, materials or styles. I'm most tickled when I try something new and it works, or when something turns out more amazing than I imagined! It's important not to view fabric as too precious to use up and enjoy. We should sew the most often with our favourite prints and colours. Savour every moment you get to look at it during the process, and then in the finished product.

Have you ever had a quilting or creative failure? What happened? What did you learn from it, if anything?

Sometimes an idea is better in my imagination than in reality. I have had grand ideas for quilting designs that I cannot figure out how to execute in the end. Usually the "failures" can be remedied by changing some fabric or colour combinations, improving contrast or rearranging the pieces into a whole new design. When I don't love a finished quilt, it usually teaches me a lesson about my process: I was too inhibited, too rigid in sticking to a plan, or conversely didn't plan enough before diving in.

What quilt traditions do you hold dear? What quilting conventions do you ignore or challenge?

I love the old tradition of using what you have. Of course, I love fabric—it's a major part of why I quilt! But it's also important to me to use fabric that I have collected over time rather than saving it. I love the look of scrappy quilts and usually incorporate as much variety as I can. Whenever possible, I like to turn the conventional idea of what is neutral on its head. That might mean using an off-beat colour for a background

fabric or using a variety of prints in the same colour family in place of just one in a pattern. I really admire quilters who are willing to make unusual combinations and it's important to me to push my comfort zone in this area, too.

In your opinion or experience, how does the act of quilting bridge the past, present and future?

Quilting is such a traditional handcraft that has evolved over time. I love that it has worldwide appeal rather than being associated with a specific culture. It's also exciting that it is now a hobby shared by grandmothers and young people alike. When I first started quilting, before the modern quilting phenomenon started, I got some funny looks when I showed up to quilting classes or groups, or told others that I enjoyed the craft.

In my own life, quilting has helped me build strong relationships. It is a major connection that I share with my mother and sister. I have also had the incredible privilege of visiting quilting guilds around the country to share my work and teach others. The vast majority of those who attend my talks and workshops are of my mother's generation and older. I enjoy these ladies a great deal and feel that I connect with them and forge friendships that defy any difference in age.

When and how did you become a professional?

I joined the blogging craze on the late side, but I wanted to join the conversation. Instagram followed. It wasn't long before the community drew me in and made me want to share more in the form of publishing patterns and teaching. I love the online quilting community for the opportunity to make friends all over the world. There is something special about belonging and knowing that others understand your obsession with things like pretty fabric and the urge to make quilts.

I wrote some early patterns and spent time learning software and developing my writing and digital illustration skills over several years. It took a lot of time to build credibility and gain a foothold, to get to a point where people bought my patterns and showed a lasting interest in what I was making and designing.

My business has evolved into a small online shop that includes the patterns I design and a few specialty rulers. I designed the Classic Curves Ruler for cutting and making curved piecing easier; it is an accomplishment that I am really proud of. My shop also carries a curated selection of fabrics that I feel have interesting, quilt-friendly prints. My favourite task is creating custom bundles of fabric to go with my patterns, giving my customers a unique mix of fabrics for making their own beautiful quilt.

What breadth of activity and responsibilities do you have as a professional quilter?

It has been important to stay active on social media, to make connections around the quilting world. One of my favourite aspects of being part of the industry is the people I've met, and opportunities to fulfill goals. There is nothing like the feeling of having something you created appear in print or be recognized by a company or designer you admire.

"Building a community around quilting is my primary goal as a business person, as well as a creative person. Part of that is building others up and bringing new members into the fold and helping them feel like they belong."

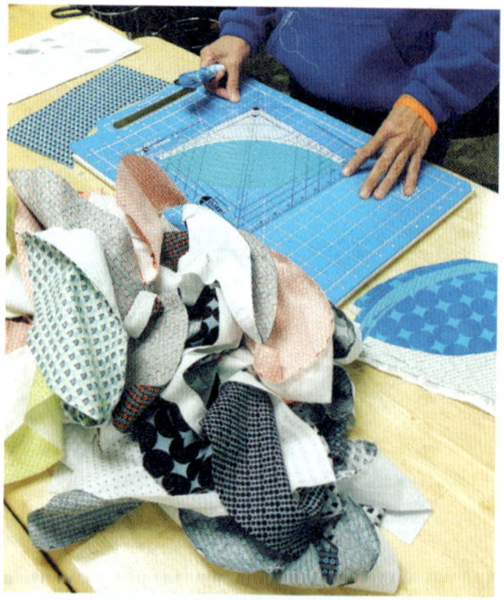

WORKSPACE

I am very blessed to occupy a spare room in our home. It is all mine and all for Color Girl Quilts: my shop inventory, where I sew my quilts and where I feel most inspired. I have two tables. One is for cutting, since I need a good bit of space for cutting yardage and preparing website shop orders to mail out. The other holds my sewing machine, another small cutting mat and (usually) stacks of fabric that I may or may not be currently using. It is a fabric lover's paradise—to me, anyway. This is also my film studio! I have recently discovered a love of making video tutorials and started a YouTube channel.

It is extremely important to me to stay true to myself. I turn down projects that are not in keeping with my aesthetic or that would be work rather than pleasure. I also have a strong desire to be a positive force in the industry. This means that I do my best to support others and be available to those who follow my social media accounts and to customers in my shop.

Are you able to support yourself in the quilt industry or do you have other endeavours as well?

I am fortunate to have the financial support of my husband so I can do my quilting business, but I do also have a part-time job. I work at the local children's hospital as a research nurse. Quilting does not provide a living wage; I do it because I really enjoy it and find fulfillment in sharing and being part of the quilting community. It's a dream to establish enough different streams within my quilting business for it to be my sole living. Maybe someday!

What motivates and inspires you?

I feel rewarded by making. The whole process motivates me and the finished product is the reward. It brings me a lot of happiness to see a quilt through from choosing the fabric and design to executing and finishing it!

I am also motivated and inspired by the people who cheer me on. I love it when a quilter shares that they made a quilt with one of my patterns or is inspired to try curved piecing because of my tutorials or my ruler, or something I've made with it.

And, of course, fabric. I always feel that I can't sew fast enough to make something with every wonderful fabric that comes along, but I can dream and enjoy all of them with my eyes or through sending them out to customers of my shop. ❄

colorgirlquilts.com
@colorgirlquilts

SHERRI LYNN WOOD

I am an artist, author and teacher. I've been improvising patchwork quilts as a creative life practice for 30 years. I have an MFA in sculpture and much of the work I do in the quilting community I see as part social practice and part creative placemaking, in the wider discipline of being a sculptor of experiences and place. My creative practice and work is my life's calling. I am deeply grateful for the opportunities I've been given to follow this calling and thrive.

I began sewing when I was 12, inspired by curtain remnants sent to me by my grandmother, who made draperies professionally. I made my first quilt at 24. At 30 I shifted from a consumer-based practice to a service-based practice. During this period I got rid of all my materials—tons of stash—fabrics, beads, dyes, etc., and began making quilts with and for people out of the clothing of loved ones who'd died. Improv patchwork and the process of hand finishing a quilt mirrors the bereavement and transformation process. At first, it was self-healing, and as I healed I made a decision to follow this trajectory and facilitate craft and quilt making as a practice that empowers and supports the agency of others.

"In improv there is no such thing as a failure or a mistake. There is no vocabulary for such, since perfection is not the goal, rather pattern exploration and discovery are."

How would you describe your style or aesthetic?

I'm an improviser, not a designer or planner. What emerges when I improvise is a reflection of the way my mind makes patterns in the present moment based on the resources—materials, skills, experience—I have at hand. My outcomes tend to be complex. My

PHOTOS BY SARAH REMINGTON FROM *THE IMPROV HANDBOOK FOR MODERN QUILTERS* (ABRAMS, 2015) USED WITH PERMISSION.

edge is choosing a simple solution over the complex. Sometimes it's messy, sometimes elegant, sometimes playful, sometimes dark. It's all a reflection of my rhythm of attention. My aesthetic is a reflection of my problem-solving mind at any given moment, and at its best my honest heart.

What are your intentions when making a quilt or starting a creative project? What thought processes do you typically go through?

Improv is a collaborative process. I try to cultivate receptive creativity that listens and responds, affirms and builds as patterns emerge and unfold during the process. I don't plan and I try my best not to control the outcomes. "Yes and" is my mantra. In order to sustain flow, I believe it's important to make creative decisions based on what I like and not on what I don't like or am critical of. "Yes and," instead of "yes but."

What quilt traditions do you hold dear? What quilting conventions do you ignore or challenge?

I'm an improviser. I am not interested in fixed pattern traditions for myself but I do respect them as a tradition beloved by many. I'm happy that today we have options, and that flexible pattern work is no longer seen or judged as being less worthy through the fixed pattern lens. The two traditions of fixed and flexible patchwork are like apples and oranges: completely different and both delicious, depending on your tastes.

In your opinion or experience, how does the act of quilting bridge the past, present and future?

I believe that the way I or anyone else makes patterns is a reflection of who we are. When paid attention to, the way we make patterns in our patchwork can reveal the way we make patterns in life and relationships.

"Finding flow and being truly creative, present and honest with yourself and your emotions are required to be a great improviser. Improv patchwork is not an escape into tedious perfection or mindless repetition, but a journey of deep self-discovery and presence."

Would you consider yourself as a professional within the quilting industry?

I am an artist by vocation. I am thankful that I've been able to earn an income by it. I am primarily a teacher and I have published one book, *The Improv Handbook For Modern Quilters* (Abrams, 2015). I see both as outreach, service, social practice and part of my work as a sculptor.

Do any particular ideas, objects or activities—outside of and unrelated to quilting—inform and inspire your quilting practice?

Systems-centred theory, music and language, composing and writing have influenced my work, particularly the work of John Cage and Eileen Miles. ✻

What motivates and inspires you?

"Patterns and living human systems, and the ways in which we can grow and heal from the things we make and do in our daily lives."

WORKSPACE

I recently moved from Oakland, California, to Cincinnati, Ohio, in order to follow my creative path full time. I'm currently between studios. I used to have a live-work warehouse loft in industrial east Oakland.

"I believe something as mundane and functional as threading a needle, when engaged intentionally or witnessed within the context of aesthetic experience, can trigger a deeper, embodied understanding of our relationship to both the concept and activity of focus. I see craft—the work of human hands in history—as containing the potential to create, by hand, new relationships inside living human systems, opening up space for personal agency and social change."

sherrilynnwood.com
@sherrilynnwood

Mother & Daughters

by **Deborah Manson**

I designed and made a quilt for each of my twin daughters as a celebration of their lives and of motherhood in 2016. Each quilt is made from a combination of hand-dyed cloth, pieces of the children's favourite outgrown clothes, and found and donated fabric. Each quilt was quilted by hand with cotton sashiko and fluorescent threads.

The compositions and colours reflect each child's distinctive personality. My daughters and I worked together on drawings, paintings and collages, on which the quilt designs are loosely based. The quilts also include fabrics we dyed together at home, and pieces of their sewing and hand quilting. My hope is that their involvement will lead to a strong sense of attachment to the quilts.

Our collaborations began the story of each quilt but I hope that the stories of these quilts will grow over time, and that they will stay with my daughters, be cared for and repaired if necessary, and perhaps be passed on and survive as heirlooms. ❇

deborahmanson.co.uk
@deborahmanson

STEPHANIE SYMNS

I was born in New Zealand and was raised in a household of makers. My grandmother taught me to sew, knit and embroider as a kid but it was always something we did for fun, not something you could base a serious career on. When the time came to go to university I didn't know anybody who had a creative job, and although I desperately wanted to go to art school I made the "practical" choice to get a management degree and began a career in industrial marketing. But I wasn't happy, and after a few years I quit and went looking for adventure in India, Nepal, Peru and Bolivia, eventually landing in London, England, for a couple of years. Following a move to Vancouver, Canada, I began producing film and TV projects as a way to inject more creativity into my work life.

After some years of producing, it was clear that facilitating the creative efforts of others wasn't enough. I decided to go back to school and study textiles at about the same time I had two kids, which had its challenges! But I loved it so much and knew that I was getting closer to my goal. I started ANTIPOD Workshop after school and it's taken several twists and turns as I try and figure out my focus. It's only recently that I feel like I'm starting to find my direction, and I'm excited to focus on art making.

What is your personal relationship or history with quilts? What draws you to them? What led you to the world of quilts?

I've always been drawn to blankets and quilts—the fact that they relate to the body both in scale and

"I'm always thinking about how to make something new—some hybrid painting/object that hasn't existed before, that takes into account the characteristics of painting and cloth, and fuses them to make something original."

PHOTOS BY BYRON DAUNCEY, TED CLARKE, ALLISON BEDA AND STEPHANIE SYMNS

function, and are also visual, intimate objects. My mother is an avid quilter and our house is filled with her gorgeous quilts. I didn't really see myself in that world for a long time, though. I don't follow patterns and I don't care about the "rules." But at school, I encountered the monoprint works of Nancy Crow and the seed was planted. It's only fairly recently that I began making quilts, when I wanted to combine my love of painting and textiles. For me, they really start with the idea of making large-scale soft paintings that you can wrap yourself up in or treat as a picture and hang on the wall.

Quilts tend to suffer at the hands of the value system of Western modernity, but it's also this that somewhat defiantly draws me to them, although this can be a double-edged sword. Through quiltmaking, we can draw on so many textile associations. It's such a rich and complex language filled with contradictions and questions of aesthetics and taste, class, culture, race and gender.

"Painted studies are translated to fabric to create works that blur the line between utility and art. The quilts explore composition, colour, scale and materiality with a respect for the rawness of the material and the imperfections inherent to hand work."

I'm particularly interested at the moment in building on the strong connections between abstract painting and textiles to delve into issues of complex ecologies, feminism, domesticity and false hierarchies. If we can champion aesthetic openness perhaps we can develop a lens through which to facilitate more inclusive attitudes in culture at large.

How would you describe your style or aesthetic?

I think I'm still working out my aesthetic—I find a lot of different types of work very appealing, but my own work tends to be abstract and explore formal concerns visually whilst embracing ideas about complex ecologies, ambiguity, labour and feminism. I'm interested in colour relationships primarily, and shape and composition. I am drawn to abstraction, which as a complex and ambiguous form is perfect for exploring the ideas that interest me. I'm very interested in exploring scale, especially in the quilts, which operate at the scale of the body, as well as repetition and shifting pattern as metaphors for lived experience. I guess I would say my aesthetic is bold and graphic, and often explores a kind of flexible, organic geometry.

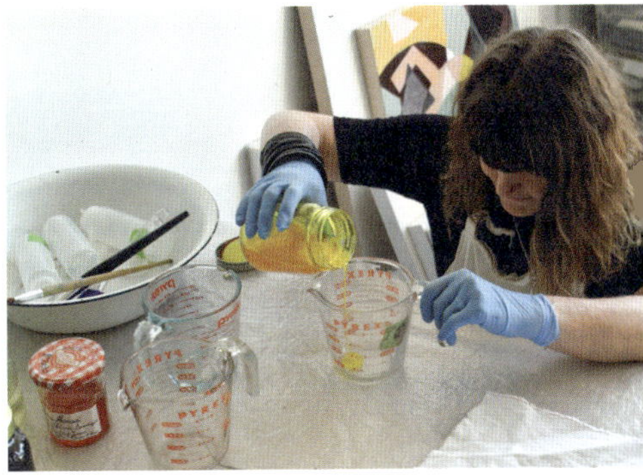

What are your intentions when making a quilt or starting a creative project? What thought processes do you typically go through?

I usually have a range of different ideas that have been percolating, so I just start with broad exploration. I often begin with image research and spend a lot of time looking at paintings and colour relationships using my own swatches. It's a fairly loose process—I do sketch out ideas using small painted studies, but I've learned that they are frequently just a starting point and that the final piece may end up somewhere else.

The next step is to start painting—either more or less to a plan. I prep the fabric, clean the studio and mix my chemicals and dyes, and then get going! I love this part of the process, it's often slow and I need to be in the right state of mind so I don't make mistakes. I'm all for happy accidents, but a big, unintended blob of dark dye can't be undone! From here on it's just about painting, steaming and rinsing to see what I've got and then responding to it. I've definitely had pieces that had to be completely reconfigured. I've learned to just breathe and figure out what needs to be done, whether it's paint more fabric or spend time just looking and shuffling things around.

What mindset or attitude do you think is best for quilting? How does quilting affect your mental and physical health?

I find that with any creative endeavour I need unpressured time and space in order to get into the mindset to actually create new work. This is difficult with young kids around and I find that I'm constantly bookended by other tasks or responsibilities. I balance this by taking a long studio day at the weekend or arranging after-school childcare once a week, and I sometimes design my own personal art residency by escaping to a cabin on my own with a trunk full of art supplies! These retreats don't happen often, but I find these times to be so rich with ideas that they fuel me for a long time.

The rest—research, thinking, writing notes, sampling and sketching—happens in the blocks of time I have during the day in my studio and at home in the evenings. The way that I make quilts means that each part of the process is quite different. Being in the studio tends to be a bit more physical, as I'm on my feet while I paint, and at home I do more computer and design work. I usually sew at home so that I can jump in and out of a project at any free moment. The variety is great for my physical health. As for my mental health, it's absolutely necessary! Making is such a part of my life and it's become increasingly apparent that it's the primary thing that keeps me sane!

Have you ever had a quilting or creative failure? What happened? What did you learn from it, if anything?

So many failures! I think it's part of the process and I don't see it as a negative. I'm not saying it doesn't get challenging but I trust that if I keep going, a little nugget will eventually reveal itself and show me how to resolve the piece. An experimental mindset and openness to ideas shifting and changing is so important.

Technically speaking, the process of painting the

fabric for my quilts has taken years to work out. There have been some real moments of (crushing) failure and I have just had to keep going and experiment with different dye recipes, fabrics and methods to arrive at a successful outcome.

From a creative perspective, when you're working out a visual vocabulary you just have to try things and then react to them. It's an iterative process where you need to be open and alert to the possibilities that present themselves at each stage of creating. My latest quilts, Echo I and II, are examples of this. I made sketches and painted the fabric but found that when I put the pieces together they just didn't work. So I painted some more pieces, put them together and they still didn't work. I decided to just cut everything up and piece it back together, and this has proven to be a fantastic discovery and a new way of working. For me, the method also speaks to the ideas I'm trying to embody in my work such as resourcefulness and embracing ambiguity and chance.

What quilt traditions do you hold dear? What quilting conventions do you ignore or challenge?

I am not married to any particular traditions or conventions but I am certainly informed by them. I research historical works and techniques for executing a piece, but am equally influenced by mathematics, scientific theories, global traditions, contemporary design and painting.

Craft is important to me, as in the mastery of my materials, but that doesn't necessarily translate to traditional ideas of perfection when it comes to things like perfect points or straight lines. Sometimes those are important and sometimes they aren't—it depends on what I'm trying to achieve with the piece. If something is supposed to be functional I will always consider those needs to be critical with regards to

"I'm interested in the way in which larger patterns can be generated from component pieces through rotation and repetition. This relates to geometry and the study of permutations, which has always seemed like a great metaphor for possibility, and one that I think brings a sense of abundance and optimism to the work."

execution, but I always challenge any convention, whether in art or life! To be perfectly honest I would like to be far looser with my work and less concerned with traditional ways of working. I'm exploring some new ideas with unfinished edges, unusual sizes and shapes, holes, nets and exposed seams. It's hard for me to let go of the "proper" way of doing things in the way that I've been taught, but I want to experiment along the continuum of functional/nonfunctional work and see what happens.

In your opinion or experience, how does the act of quilting bridge the past, present and future?

Broadly speaking, textiles have a complex legacy and that's what draws me to them. Quilts and quilting have a history that goes back potentially thousands of years, from Egypt and many other parts of the world to medieval quilted garments to kantha, Hmong patchwork, Japanese sashiko and the Sicilian Tristan quilt of around 1360, to what is now often claimed as a uniquely American tradition. I'm interested in this complex history and how it shines a light on industrialization, globalization, gender roles, technology and cultural channels. Any quilts that we make are part of this complicated and evolving soup of influences, traditions and varying cultural frames of reference.

Personally speaking, making quilts binds me to the past through my mother and grandmother, to feminist histories, to global textile traditions and art making. I'm particularly interested in the domestic, from both a historical perspective and in terms of my own experiences as a feminist with two small kids who has found herself in a frankly surprisingly traditional domestic arrangement. I love the idea of quilts acting as a bridge through time to other artists, and between ideas I'm exploring now, including my personal relationship to craft, art, time and labour.

Would you consider yourself as a professional within the quilting industry? When and how did you become a professional?

I am still very new to the world of quilts but I consider them to be a growing part of my design and art practice. I would consider that I became a "professional" when I sold my first quilt and then when my work was shown at Fluevog in their Gastown flagship store as part of the annual show Crafted Vancouver. My work has subsequently been shown in *Interior Design* magazine online and I'm currently planning a new body of work for exhibition and sale.

I'm currently making and selling my quilts online. I am working on my surface pattern design portfolio and aspire to release a line of quilt fabrics.

Are you able to support yourself in the quilt industry or do you have other endeavours as well?

I don't currently support myself through work in the quilt industry, although I hope to in part through sales, commissions, workshops and fabric designs. I sell a line of textile soft goods and am working on a portfolio of surface pattern designs for licensing for release in the near future.

What motivates and inspires you?

I am inspired by patterns, artwork, nature, science, mathematics, cultural mark-making traditions, travel and fashion. I am naturally curious about the world so I read a lot about a wide range of topics and I'm lucky to have a lot of clever, creative friends who also inspire me. I'm reading in a more focused way at the moment about abstraction, surface pattern design, textile histories and essays on quilts—I'm really interested in being able to locate my work within a framework of complicated histories and contemporary practice. ✻

WORKSPACE

I am really lucky to have found a great light-filled studio space with a high ceiling in Vancouver that I share with three other artists. I need a studio outside my house because the quilt painting takes up a lot of space. Also, you can't really use the dyes I paint with in a domestic space, as they're toxic in powder form, so I tend to do my wet and messy work in the studio.

I have an office at home where I can do admin work, and work on my surface pattern design and smaller paintings. I do tend to spread out, though, and have been known to overtake the dining room too, especially when I'm sewing a quilt. I'm lucky that we are all makers, so spreading out is part of our modus operandi at home.

My studio is about a half-hour walk from home and I love the chance to get some fresh air and get into a good headspace before I arrive. It really helps set up the day.

Having a shared space outside the house is magical.

antipodworkshop.com
@antipodworkshop

TARA FAUGHNAN

I am a professional freelance textile designer and quilter living and working in Oakland, California. I started to quilt around 2001 or so, using as my guide a reprint of the 1931 edition of *101 Patchwork Patterns* by Ruby Short McKim. I had no idea such things as rotary cutters, plastic templates and freezer paper existed. I spent many happy weeks tracing around cardboard templates and cutting out my pieces with a pair of scissors.

Somewhere along the way, my love of quilting led me to school and on to a career in textile design, with clients including Michael Miller Fabrics and Pottery Barn Kids. I find inspiration in forms, shapes and the place where two seams meet. Colour interaction is the key inspiration that drives me. It's that intuitive moment when you put two colours together, and then two more, and two more after that that I focus on. The explorations are endless and I strive to try to walk the line of discomfort and still make everything work together as a whole.

I draw a lot of inspiration from the simple bold geometry of antique quilts, the gorgeous bright colours from textiles around the world, and the freedom and spontaneity found in unconventional and improvisationally pieced quilts. When I look at my current work, I see all three of these aspects represented. I like to use simple geometry and complex colour interaction, and find that the line exists somewhere between harmony and discord.

"I generally start with a shape that I want to explore. I find it fascinating to take a simple triangle, for example, and notice how I respond to the shape just by altering its dimensions slightly. I like to use repeating blocks and shapes so that I am free to really explore colour and begin to play with how I can disrupt the pattern using value as well."

What is your personal relationship or history with quilts? What draws you to them? What led you to the world of quilts?

I can tell you how I started quilting, but I've never been truly sure why. My mom is a quilter and I was introduced to them as a child both at home and out in the world. Though I have no memory of it, apparently I was drawn to an exhibit of quilts at the Oakland Museum and wanted to go see the show over and over. So I guess I've been drawn to quilts my entire life—whether it was for the geometric shapes or the tactile nature I couldn't say. I was bitten by the quilting bug as soon as I started to cut fabric for my first quilt. Completely obsessed, I would wake up at dawn and start quilting until I couldn't go any longer. I think I finished that quilt in about three weeks. It then took me three years to actually get it quilted. The quilting of a top has remained my least favourite part of the whole process.

How would you describe your style or aesthetic?

I would say that my style is traditional. I also dabble in art quilts, though, and have recently become interested in using fusible web. I think most people describe me as a modern quilter, but I'm fine with whatever style someone sees when they look at my quilts.

What mindset or attitude do you think is best for quilting? How does quilting affect your mental and physical health?

One of the best things I've done for my quilting practice is to constantly tell myself it's okay to fail. I'm also working on focusing on the process rather than the product. I've just gone through a six-month creative rut where I got really stuck on the end product. I wanted to try new things, got stuck on the fear of failure and forgot about the joy of the process. I have not mastered this but it's something that I'm working towards.

In general, I design my quilts very quickly by laying out pieces on the design wall, letting one decision

affect the next. I usually don't go back and change the layout, as I love the weird parts of a design that come about in the initial process when you are not over-thinking it but letting it evolve.

Have you ever had a quilting or creative failure? What happened? What did you learn from it, if anything?

I have plenty of creative and quilting failures. What happens is the bits go into my garbage can and if I'm not wild about the top but don't want to give it away, it just gets folded up and put on the shelf. Occasionally I

just give away quilt tops that I'm no longer interested in. I've learned over the years that I must have failures because that means I'm taking risks. I've noticed that I need to follow an idea whether it's successful or not. And often my most exciting ideas come after a "failure." I try to look at it not so much as a failure as I just made something that I wasn't wild about, and that just led to the next idea. If I constantly second guess myself on what ideas will work or not, then I will never begin new ideas.

"Skinny tall triangles have a lot of tension and energy, and when you shorten the triangle and make the angles less severe it begins to feel calmer."

What quilt traditions do you hold dear? What quilting conventions do you ignore or challenge?

They are one and the same for me. Precision. I tried to hide it for years but I really am excited about points that line up. I'm not a perfectionist, so I give it my best shot and if it doesn't line up, I don't rip it out. I always figure I'll do better on the next one, and there is too much to do to rip out something that's already been sewn up. That being said, the design of the quilt, it's impact and the effect it has on me as I'm creating it, and later on, on the viewer when I put it out in the world, is so much more important to me than whether or not the points match. I do not think construction techniques should be more valued than design. In quilting shows, that is often the case, and I find that the winning quilts, though technically amazing, fall a bit flat for me in the design. I want there to be something unpredictable in a quilt, something that makes me wonder why the maker did what she did. I want my eyes to be surprised.

In your opinion or experience, how does the act of quilting bridge the past, present and future?

I started to become really aware of this connection when I began to do handwork, both hand piecing and hand quilting. I felt connected in a very real and profound way to all the thousands of women who had come before me; who had sat down at the end of the day with a needle and thread and began to sew. I wondered if we thought about some of the same things; I wondered if they looked forward to the nightly sewing and quilting as much as I did. I noticed how the feel of the slow stitch-by-stitch connected me to the creation more deeply than the speed of sewing by machine could. When I look at an old quilt that is hand pieced or quilted, there is a presence in the stitches that infuses the quilt with life.

Would you consider yourself as a professional within the quilting industry? When and how did you become a professional?

I have a bit of a different perspective, as I am employed as a textile designer within the quilting industry, as well as being a teacher and pattern writer.

When I started quilting in 2001, the thought of designing quilt fabrics led me to textile design school in 2007. Happily, I was unaware that there really weren't

any fabric manufacturers in the Bay Area, as I might not have gone through school. I was lucky enough to get a position working in-house with Michael Miller in their Sonoma, California, studio, where I worked with the co-owner and creative director Kathy Miller. During the nearly 10 years I worked there, I learned an incredible amount about design, colour and value, and we spent many long and happy hours discussing the ins and outs and changes happening in the industry and in quilting in general. For the most part, I kept my quilting practice separate from my job, doing an occasional quilt pattern for customer use. In the last few years, I started branching out—teaching and writing patterns, and last year I launched a subscription pattern and fabric club with Sewtopia that's been going really well. I do occasional work for other fabric companies as well, doing in-house textile design.

What breadth of activity and responsibilities do you have as a professional quilter?

Teaching is a good part of my income. Pattern sales are the other avenue, though at this point I don't market them very much, as I'm still on the fence about if this is a road I really want to go down. Occasionally I do commission pieces, but I set my prices high, so I only make a few a year for people who see the value in what I do. Last year I had the amazing opportunity to design quilts for a hotel, but that still won't open for at least another year. When that launches I will look into more commercial opportunities. I am okay with taking things slowly and letting my quilting career evolve in a natural way. It's taken me a lot longer to get to the point of making money from quilting, but I've been able to do it my way.

WORKSPACE

I have a spare bedroom in our house, though I think I really need another room as well—craft hoarding is seriously alive and well here. When I started sewing I only had a drafting table to set up my machine on, so I learned how to sew standing up. I have my ironing board next to me, and I cut and sew on the large drafting table. I think it's really much more convenient than having to sit to sew and then stand up to cut and iron. I use IKEA bookshelves to store my stash but have two closets full of old fabrics and projects, various boxes of zippers and assorted crafting supplies. I have definitely caught the destash bug that is going around but haven't found the time yet to dive into that endeavour. I dream of a minimalist sewing studio that is totally organized and peaceful, but the reality is I'm a chaotic and messy creator, and I feel stilted trying to stay neat and organized. Piles of fabric jumbled together have lead to great and unexpected colour choices!

Are you able to support yourself in the quilt industry or do you have other endeavours as well?

Most of my income comes from my day job. If I was dependent on making income solely from quilting patterns or teaching, it would be really tough, as I've just started down this road in the last few years and have been taking it pretty slow.

What motivates and inspires you?

This is actually a really hard question for me to answer, and not one I've spent a lot of time thinking about. I sew because I am not a happy person without a creative outlet. I don't necessarily think or plan in words so much as I have a feeling I'd like to convey, and can best do that during the act of designing and creating. Quilting is really not a very cerebral process for me, it's kind of the opposite—a time when I can just stop thinking and just be.

Do any particular ideas, objects or activities—outside of and unrelated to quilting—inform and inspire your quilting practice?

I think being a textile designer has had a huge impact on my quilting, especially in the use of colour. I have to constantly work with colours and palettes that are not a personal favourite, but I recognize when the colours are working together and how to adjust something to create more cohesion or pop in a palette. It's an incredible lesson to work with colours you don't personally like and to still see that they work successfully together. I think this has really allowed me to open up my own palette. ❇

tarafaughnan.com
@tarafaughnan

PEACE

Peace / Piece

by **Emma Anna**

emmaannaportfolio.wixsite.com

Born in Australia, I now live on the Caribbean Coast of Colombia. After work in journalism and graphic design, I embarked on a career in public art. In the time that I have been living in Colombia, the government has negotiated a peace treaty after a 60-year civil war. I have begun to play with the idea of peace/piece, and of collaborative patchwork quilts as a means of memorializing the conflict.

I teach patchwork to adults and children, and have produced several community peace quilts in Colombia and my native Australia. While quilting was once a tradition passed through generations, hand sewing is not a technique that is necessarily taught to today's younger generations. I enjoy empowering children and people of my own generation with this skill.

In Colombia I am the co-director of La Casa Verde, a multipurpose event and arts venue in the city of Barranquilla. Our key mission is to educate the local community about contemporary art practice and to promote the arts and artists of our region. We view the creative potential of the human imagination as a tool for social and political change.

I am concerned about broader political issues such as racism and peace making. There is evidence of this in the quilts I make—the mixing of fabrics and patterns, and the idea of "pieces" being formed into "peace." I am also interested in community building and work as an artist in the public realm to produce projects that unite and inspire diverse publics. I only use a hexagon form in my quilts. To me this shape is reminiscent of the life of bees. Like worker bees, we all need to strive together to build solid homes and vital futures. ✻

TRICIA ROYAL

I am a 44-year-old textile artist, wife and mother of one daughter. I live in Sherman Oaks, California. I am originally from the Orlando, Florida, metro area. I've lived all over the United States, with stops in New York City, San Francisco and the greater Bay Area, and Chicago over the years. I studied art history at the University of North Florida, and fashion design at Parsons the New School for Design. I have been sewing since the age of 11; my grandmother, Josephine, taught me how to sew the summer before sixth grade. We made a pink linen straight skirt as my first project. I have been collecting vintage clothing and housewares since high school, with a particular focus on garments and objects from the 1960s, '70s and '80s. I have had a regular studio quilt practice for a decade.

PORTRAIT BY LORI ROSE, SIGNATURE IMAGES, INC., CAMPBELL, CA

What is your personal relationship or history with quilts? What draws you to them? What led you to the world of quilts?

There weren't any quilts in my home growing up; I became aware of the craft in adulthood. I've been an avid thrift shopper since my teens, and over the years I have amassed a sizable hoard of 1970s craft books, many of which feature quilts. Something about the homespun, patchwork-infused aesthetic of the '70s really resonated with me. Later, after college and years of self-study, I came to understand that quilts are primarily a craft practiced by women (at least historically), and that quilts and quiltmaking may be seen as a feminist expression, that quiltmaking may be seen as a feminist act. I believe that quilts deserve respect as art objects. I also just really love the way that quilts look, how seemingly simple tessellations and blocks can serve as a means for endless play and personalization.

> "I see myself as part of a long line of women who have made textiles, an unbroken thread that stretches back through the millennia. Textiles have always been an integral part of everyday life, from cradle to grave."

How would you describe your style or aesthetic?

Graphic, lots of patterning. Right now I am really into neons. I really like to turn up the volume, especially when it comes to colour and saturation—a purposeful power clash. In my quilt work and body of textile work overall, I like to investigate the liminal space between past and present, chaos and control, trash and treasure. I like to challenge the viewer's mind regarding matters of taste and see how far I can push the limits. What this usually means is I like to put wild prints next to each other and see what happens. If it gives my mind a zing and feels right to me, I go with it.

I make art quilts: quilts meant for display. Right now I am doing a lot of experimentation with surface design: dyeing and hand-printing fabrics (with silkscreen, relief printing, monoprint and found-object techniques). I am using those handmade fabrics (along with solids) in my quilts almost exclusively, rather than relying on commercially available designer fabrics.

What are your intentions when making a quilt or starting a creative project? What thought processes do you typically go through?

Ideas often come to me just before bed, or as I am drifting off to sleep. I see each quilt as an exploration, or another iteration of an idea or path I've explored before—working out variations. One idea often leads to the next. Sometimes this process is linear, other times it's like a flow chart with multiple paths to follow. I tend to work on five to ten quilts at once, going hard at one quilt for a while, setting it aside to chase another idea, and then circling back to work on another. Eventually, pieces do come to fruition, but some quilts may take years to complete. I often work in different tracks: some pieces that are more complex and patterned, and others that are more simple, and kind of brainless.

How does quilting affect your mental and physical health?

My artmaking and quilting practice have a huge impact on my mental well-being. I'm an introvert, and have had periods of profound depression and anxiety over the years; quilting or spending time in my garage painting and printing on fabrics acts as a balm for my soul and helps me get into a calming state of flow, functioning something like an antidepressant. I function better with ample alone time and crave the relative serenity and simplicity of my studio and my regular practice. My partner and daughter are very understanding and supportive of my needs and my art, and know I'm a better mom and wife if I am given ample time in my studios.

"I use a lot of vintage fabrics in my quilts; reuse and recycling are really important to me, on an ethical level. We live in such a throwaway culture."

Have you ever had a quilting or creative failure? What happened? What did you learn from it, if anything?

I fail all the time! If you're going to embrace experimentation and innovation as an ethos, you've got to expect that failures will (and do!) occur. Mistakes are lessons and can lead to further innovation and discovery. It's important to be open and set up situations where you can control what you can control, and let some things be left to chance. It's a mindset of willingness and openness. If you let yourself become paralyzed by a fear that you'll make mistakes, you'll never get anything done and you'll kill your creative spark.

What quilt traditions do you hold dear? What quilting conventions do you ignore or challenge?

I am deeply interested in the tradition and history of quilts and quiltmaking, and the people who made them and make them today. I often use traditional blocks as a jumping-off point for my quilts, and many of my quilts are block-based; I see this as a nod to the past while I simultaneously try to forge my own path and give these blocks my own personal spin. I want to reference the past and push things forward at the same time. My use of secondhand fabric is a reference to the use of scraps in the centuries-long tradition of quiltmaking, but it's also relevant to our current times, an important paradigm we need to embrace as we deal with the environmental challenges our planet is facing. Recycling—then, as now—is a must and a moral imperative.

What motivates and inspires you?

Urban spaces and their layers and colours are very stimulating to me, and I love taking walks in cities and taking in everything I see: creative outfits on people in the street, architecture, the green spaces, accidental colour juxtapositions, commercial signage, and the irreverence, imperfection and humour of the everyday world. The energy of cities is invigorating to me, and I hope some of the influence of that urban energy comes through in my colour pairings or motifs, even if the connection is not immediately evident.

I am also very into contemporary art, feminist art and postmodern art. I love visiting art museums when I travel. I am very into the concept of remix culture, hip hop and graffiti/street art: the brash, in-your-face nature of those art forms affects me viscerally. I want to make quilts that make the viewer feel the way listening to hip hop makes me feel. ❇

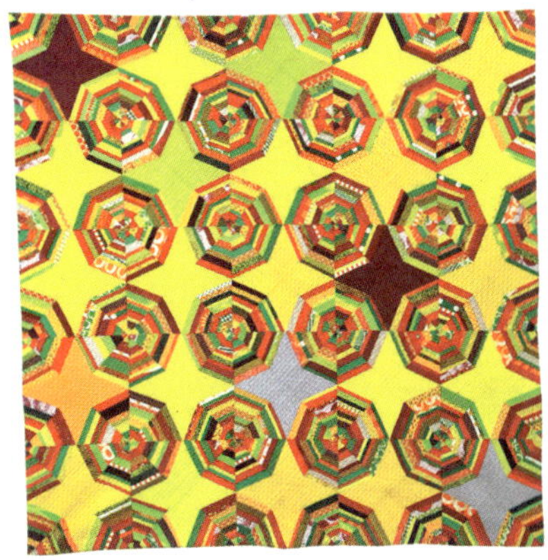

What mindset or attitude do you think is best for quilting?

"Openness to experimentation, to failure, to letting ideas flow. Openness and willingness to show up and make work, even when it feels weird. Openness to new ideas, to sharing. Close-mindedness can lead to stagnation, on both a personal and public level. I don't think openness is innate, but it can become second nature with practice."

bitsandbobbins.com
@bitsandbobbins
ART
QUILTS
=
ART
QUILTS

WORKSPACE

Until quite recently, I had three distinct spaces devoted to my studio practice: a very small sewing room with a built-in desk and bookshelves, as well as a combined sewing machine/ cutting table and a large ironing station; another bedroom where I stored my fabric and yarn stash (I also weave, knit and crochet), my loom and my longarm (a Handi-Quilter Avanté on a 10-foot frame); and a corner of my garage, where I stored my inks, paints and printing tools. In the latter, I also had a sink and lots of storage for miscellaneous art and craft supplies. It wasn't the prettiest space (I had to share space with the car, bikes, tools and luggage!) but it was functional, and I was grateful to have it. When the weather was nice I would open up the garage door super wide and let in the California sunshine and mild weather. I just moved to Los Angeles; my new home in Sherman Oaks has a sunroom off the back of the house with windows on two sides, rose bushes, lush privacy hedges and fruit trees all around. The plan is to use that lovely light-filled room as a sewing and quilting studio.

ZAK FOSTER

When I first told my partner's grandma, the first quilter I ever knew, that I was interested in learning how to quilt, she grabbed my arm, looked me dead in the eye, and said, "Buddy, you don't know how much fun you're gonna have." And it's true! I've been having a blast ever since. I've been quilting for nearly a decade now, and it's been more fun and more rewarding than I could have imagined.

I made my first quilt in the third grade for Little House on the Prairie Day. It was a simple four-square patch that I later turned into a pillow. I didn't make another quilt for over a decade, but that little quilt must have planted a seed, because I picked it back up in college, when I made my first bed-size quilt. I used a few old sheets (repurposing, even then!), but I became disheartened when I couldn't make all my corners line up. I thought a good quilt had to be a perfect square. I didn't sew again for another decade. And then I saw my first Gee's Bend quilts, and I was so inspired that I haven't stopped making quilts since.

"I'm drawn to found materials because in addition to knowing that my art has helped reclaim perfectly usable resources, working with nontraditional fabrics imposes certain limitations on the design process that I find propel me to do more meaningful and interesting work."

What is your personal relationship or history with quilts? What draws you to them? What led you to the world of quilts?

Quilting was one of the earliest zero-waste art forms, and I believe this was one of the first things that attracted me to it, even if I wasn't fully aware of that at the time. As quilters are becoming more and more conscious of the abundant resources all around us in the form of materials that can be repurposed—things like old clothes, worn-out bed sheets, stained tablecloths—we are drawing on a long tradition of making do, finding creative ways to be

content with what we already have. This is incredibly encouraging to me in the face of so much production and consumption.

I'm also interested in practicality. Quilts have an aesthetic value, but they also have utility. As a quilter, I'm not just concerned with the way quilts look, I'm also designing for comfort, warmth, security and memory. I think about this with every quilt I make.

How would you describe your style or aesthetic?

I come from North Carolina, with its long history of textile manufacturing, and I'm currently living in Brooklyn, New York. I attribute my aesthetic to a blend of the two places. The South has given us some of the world's most remarkable quilts. So many of us quilting today have drawn our inspiration from the quilters of Gee's Bend, Alabama, and we owe that community a huge debt of gratitude for the way they've helped us see what's possible with textiles. Living in a place like New York, one is constantly surrounded with inspiration in the form of architecture, the fine arts, textiles

from around the world, those hip kids just being hip kids. I feel like walking down the street fills my inner artistic well (as Julia Cameron would say) with so much fodder for design that the city can't help but express itself through my work. I see this especially in the movement I aim to build into my designs, along with bold and at times unexpected colour palettes.

What are your intentions when making a quilt or starting a creative project? What thought processes do you typically go through?

I rarely have an overall design mapped out in my head when I start a new project. I begin with a few scraps of fabric whose colours, patterns or textures complement one another, and go from there, piecing them together until I find an arrangement that is somehow surprising, intriguing or unexpected. Working with repurposed materials is a great way to push yourself creatively to discover new shape and colour combinations. Process-wise, one of the most helpful things I ever did was build a design wall: a couple of pieces of

"My favourite quilts are the ones that tell stories."

foam insulation with a white flannel sheet wrapped around them. Being able to step back and see a composition from a distance lets me see more clearly what's working and what's not working. Another trick I use to evaluate composition is to take a picture of the quilt top. When I can see it reduced down to a two-inch square on my phone, a lot of times I'll notice something new that I can't see when I look at it in real size.

What mindset or attitude do you think is best for quilting? How does quilting affect your mental and physical health?

Gentleness and unhurriedness (if I may invent a word) are essential to how I work. If I've had a rough day or I'm feeling down on myself, that's usually not the best time to start a new project. Improv work requires risk taking, and risk taking assumes you'll make a few mistakes along the way. If I'm tired or stressed out, not only will I be more irritated when I have to rip out yet another seam, but more importantly, I won't be able to see the moments of accidental beauty that can only be perceived when one's creative eye is wide open. Stress and self-criticism shut that eye. That being said, if I've had a rough day and I'm in the middle of a project—that is, I already know my basic direction for the quilt—then working with fabrics can be a balm. I often feel recharged after time spent with fabric in my hands.

Have you ever had a quilting or creative failure? What happened? What did you learn from it, if anything?

I've definitely finished quilt tops that I looked at a week later and wondered what in the world I was thinking. I've got about half a dozen quilt tops folded away in the closet that will probably never get made into quilts for that very reason. I keep waiting for a creative solution that might somehow tie them all together. More than not liking a quilt, though, what I struggle with more is times when I'm not inspired, when no two fabrics ever look good together, and sewing each seam feels like a Sisyphean task. My usual remedy is to gently push through. I find that if I can just work for a good hour or so, usually I can recover my momentum and inspiration, but sometimes that's easier said than done.

What quilt traditions do you hold dear? What quilting conventions do you ignore or challenge?

My favourite quilts are the ones that tell stories. A couple of summers ago, I had the opportunity to see the world's oldest surviving quilt. The Victoria and Albert Museum in London has the Tristan and Isolde quilt, which was made eight centuries ago in Italy and which tells the story of the pair's star-crossed love affair. It's a whole-cloth quilt that has wads of cotton stuffed between two layers of white linen for a trapunto effect, and a mesmerizing number of tiny hand stitches. The handiwork itself is astounding enough, but then you start to read the story embroidered into the quilt, and become immersed at a whole new level. What I love is that there's more than one way for a quilt to have a story. Sometimes it's the origin story of the fabric. Sometimes it's the process. But I'm convinced that it's the narrative of a quilt that takes it beyond just something pretty to put on your bed and into the realm of art (which you still might end up putting on your bed!).

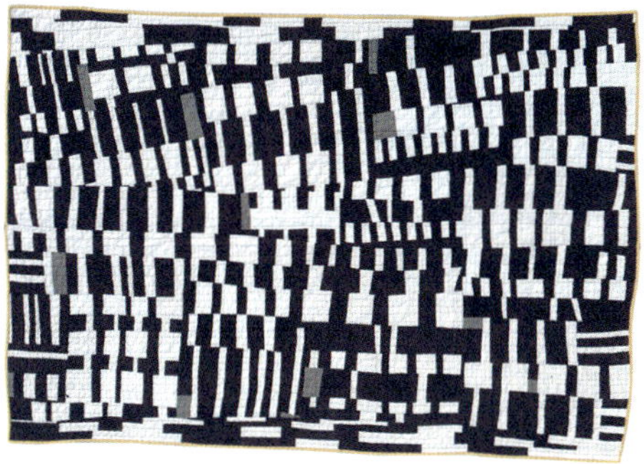

I would love to see more quilts made when quilters trusted their gut, whatever that means for them. Maybe it means we sew our first improv quilt, or decide not to use store-bought fabric in perfectly curated colour collections. Maybe it means our corners don't all line up just so, or we don't hide our knots. Maybe our quilts can be a little wobbly and not perfect squares.

In your opinion or experience, how does the act of quilting bridge the past, present and future?

I wish I came from a long line of quilters. The closest I come is Mamaw, my partner's grandmother. She and I first bonded over quilts on my first Thanksgiving home with him, and as a gay man meeting a houseful of family for the first time, I was happy for that point of connection. I remember Mamaw took me by the hand, pushed past the numerous aunts, uncles, nieces, nephews and dogs, and led me back to the hall closet, where there were shelves of folded and stacked quilts that she had made over the years. One by one, she took each quilt out, ran her fingers down the hand stitching and called the name of the sister who had helped her sew that particular part. At that point in my career,

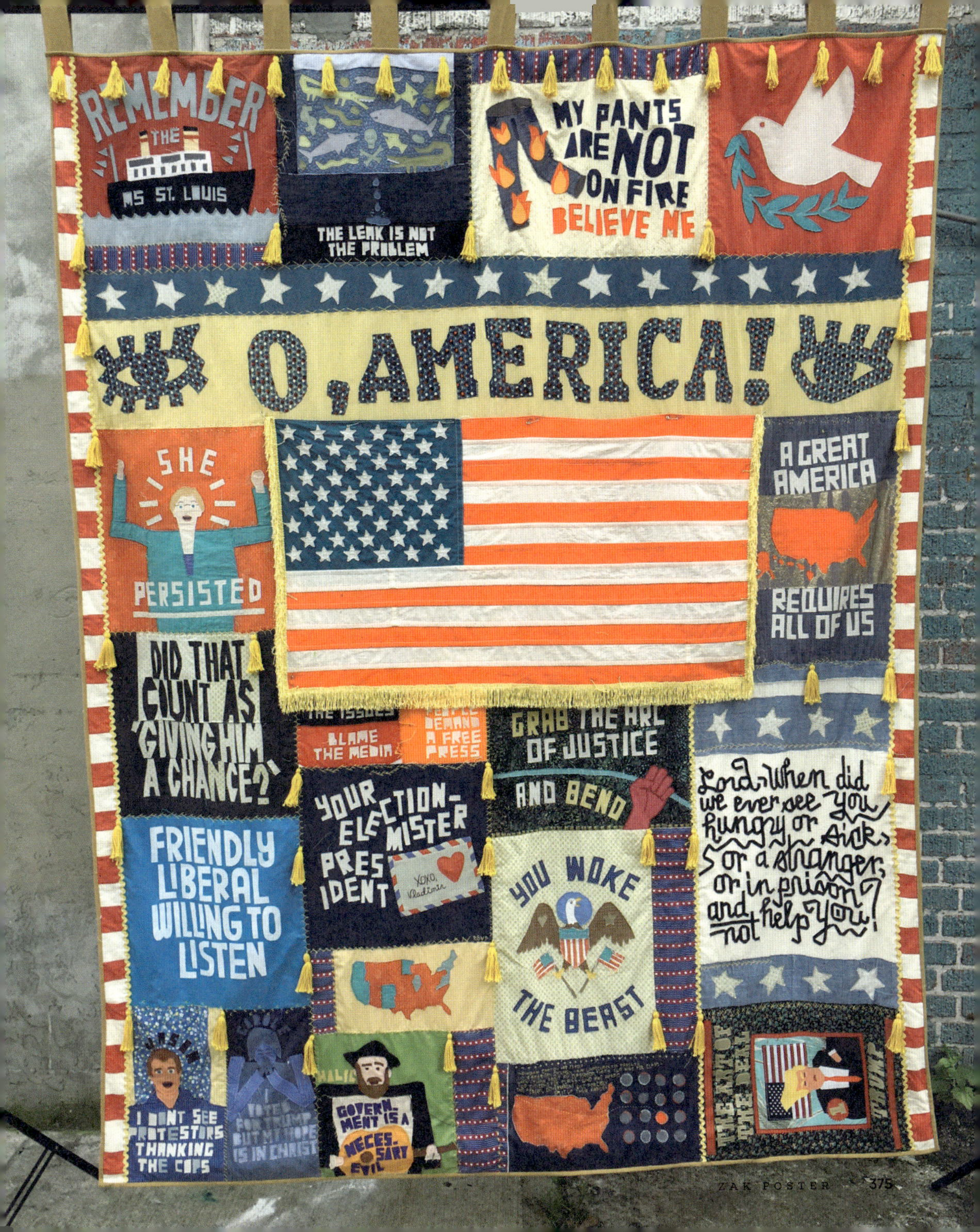
REMEMBER THE
MS ST. LOUIS
THE LEAK IS NOT THE PROBLEM
MY PANTS ARE NOT ON FIRE
BELIEVE ME
O, AMERICA!
SHE
PERSISTED
A GREAT AMERICA
REQUIRES ALL OF US
DID THAT COUNT AS 'GIVING HIM A CHANCE?'
BLAME THE MEDIA
PEOPLE DEMAND A FREE PRESS
GRAB THE ARC OF JUSTICE
AND BEND
Lord, When did we ever see you hungry or sick, or a stranger, or in prison? and not help you?
FRIENDLY LIBERAL WILLING TO LISTEN
YOUR ELECTION-MISTER PRES IDENT
XOXO, Vladimir
YOU WOKE THE BEAST
I DONT SEE PROTESTORS THANKING THE COPS
VOTED FOR TRUMP BUT MY HOPE IS IN CHRIST
GOVERN-MENT IS A NECES-SARY EVIL

> "Far more important than considering myself a professional, is acknowledging that I'm an artist... But a shift happened when I started working on pieces that were more personally significant."

I hadn't done a lot of quilting, let alone hand sewing, and the fact that years later she could still see the hand behind the stitches left a deep impression on me. Mamaw passed away a few years ago, but I still have the quilt she gave me, and when I wrap up in it, it's like she's still around, keeping me company. That's a bridge to the past as real as any.

Would you consider yourself as a professional within the quilting industry? When and how did you become a professional?

If I had to pick a time when I started considering myself a professional, it was probably when I realized I needed a longarm machine to produce the kind of quilts I wanted to produce. It was then that I realized that I was ready to commit to this art form

in a more substantial way. For me, though, far more important than considering myself a professional is acknowledging that I'm an artist. That took far longer. There was a time when I wouldn't venture past the title of quilter when somebody asked about my work. But a shift happened when I started working on pieces that were more personally significant. Around the time that I made a quilt on the Syrian refugee crisis, and then soon after that, when I organized a communal quilting project to bring awareness to the 43 Mexican students who disappeared one night in 2014, I realized that I had something to say as a quilter. Since then, I've been able to call myself an artist without hesitation.

WORKSPACE

Establishing a quilting empire in a one-bedroom Brooklyn apartment has been tricky. (This is an opportune moment to mention just how supportive my partner is!) I've been able to set up shop in our eat-in kitchen nook that measures about 7 feet by 11 feet. I've also got a longarm machine that takes up a good chunk of our bedroom. It's cozy. I've had to be really intentional about how I use my space, and that starts with how much fabric I allow myself to bring home. I've got one chest of drawers where I keep all my cut-up shirts and quilting fabric, and I try not to let that spill over. Once it fills up, I stop bringing home any more fabric until I've made some room. My cutting table is also my ironing table. I still iron on the same miniature dorm-room ironing board that I've had for nearly 20 years now. My favourite iron is a little travel iron. Space is tight, but it keeps me from indulging my fabric-hoarding tendencies.

What breadth of activity and responsibilities do you have as a professional quilter?

Although I currently work a full-time job—I've been a high-school teacher for 18 years—I am planning a transition to full-time quilting in the near future: a future that includes natural dyes, some agriculture and finding new ways in incorporate quilts in our lives.

For the moment, the bulk of my professional activity revolves around working on quilt commissions. I've done workshops in the past on improv quilting, hand sewing and the creative process, and it's something I would like to do more of in the future. I also really enjoy thinking about communal sewing projects. When I organized the 43 for 43 Protest Banner project, I saw how eager people were to collaborate, and how much power we have collectively, and it has inspired me to do more. I'm currently mulling over a project that would get quilters in blue states working with quilters in red states. I believe that what we have in common is far greater than what we might not agree on, but given the national dialogue recently, it doesn't always feel like that. I'm convinced that quilting can be a small but significant part of the solution. A quilt is the perfect illustration of the idea that the whole is greater than the sum of its parts, because in quilting, a few worthless scraps of fabric are somehow transformed into something much greater. We could use a little of that magic in America right now. ✻

zakfoster.com
@zakfoster.quilts

here because
something.

Native American Starquilt

by **Tsoniki Crazy Bull**

"Being generous is passed down, and I learned to give these gifts with a good heart. The effort we put into giving things to others is rewarded with the thanks they give to us, either for helping in a time of great sorrow or kindly gifting a handmade item. Passing along these skills and qualities is one way I can continue to honour my grandma."

I was lucky enough to grow up next door to a grandma who made fresh bread every day. My grandparents owned a store and she made pies and bread daily, which carried over to life after the store. If you timed your arrival just right, you could walk in the door the moment she was taking the bread out of the oven. It took every ounce of patience to wait for the bread to cool enough to slice, to enjoy that first bite with just enough melted butter.

My grandma, Vera "Tootie" Compton, was born in a small community on the Rosebud Indian Reservation. By the time I was a young girl, she was spending her summers sitting in the shade in the hot South Dakota sun, waving flies from the corn she was drying.

Native Americans are industrious people. Many say this and often what people see is the final result—the meal at a powwow, beadwork on regalia, a starquilt. What isn't seen is the work—the summer drying corn, late nights, callused fingers working on last-minute regalia, sewing at the kitchen table, and kids sitting nearby.

When I was a little girl I would sit with my grandma and sew. I'm sure it was a matter of attempting to guide fabric while she worked the presser foot, but I sat with her the same way I sat with my mom, and the same way my children sit with me. My youngest, now nine

years old, knows how to run my sewing machine because he is so focused on wanting to learn details. (He is learning beadwork, something my grandma also taught me.)

This is how our children learn—by sitting at our sides. In Native American families, we come together in times of need to create. When there is a funeral, family members make starquilts that will be given away after the services. Grandmas are not only teaching their relatives how to make a quilt from start to finish but teaching them what to do for your family when a loved one dies. It is a time of sadness from missing them, and joy from telling stories, but the younger generations remember so it can continue to be passed on. We also gift starquilts to new babies and for birthdays, graduations, weddings and other occasions.

Being generous is passed down, and I learned to give these gifts with a good heart. The effort we put into giving things to others is rewarded with the thanks they give to us, either for helping in a time of great sorrow or kindly gifting a handmade item. Passing along these skills and qualities is one way I can continue to honour my grandma. ❇

mebeingcrafty.com
@tsoniki

PHOTOS BY HEIDI STAPLES, BILL VOLCKENING